The distinction between a mountain and a molehill is your perspective.

"*Sermon on the Molehill* is a most special book. It is an inspirational treasure for anyone looking for affirmative, yet insightful, teachings about living a more peaceful and gratifying life. Rev. Cathy Jean Norman and Dr. Noelle Nelson have created a wonderful, relatable road map to a life of Peace, Joy, Balance and Harmony. And, it is a really delightful read!"

—**Rev. Elizabeth Rann Arrott,**
co-author of the award-winning book
Shortcut to a Miracle

"*Sermon on the Molehill* is absolutely excellent! It is an indispensable guide that will open doors to ever richer depths. Truly, it is never dull and often provocative. A must read!"

—**Rev. Dr. John Strickland,**
author of *Think, Feel, Heal* and a recipient of
"The Light of God Expressing"
Award from the Worldwide Unity Movement

"I have had the high honor to know Rev. Cathy Jean Norman for almost 40 years. I respect and admire her as an advanced spiritual teacher. In the new book, *Sermon on the Molehill*, she and Dr. Noelle Nelson collaborate to offer what Rev. Cathy does best in a prolific, enjoyable, highly readable presentation for readers everywhere. I highly recommend this for your spiritual growth."

—**Christopher Ian Chenoweth,**
founder PositiveChristianity.org

"With their upbeat, humorous and somewhat irreverent style, Reverend Cathy Jean Norman and Dr. Noelle Nelson skillfully guide the reader to the most important discovery we can make: how to remember and renew our all-important connection to Spirit, the very source of guidance and love. Their book is for anyone wanting a more fulfilling and peaceful way of life."

—**May L. McCarthy,**
entrepreneur, investor and author of
The Path to Wealth and The Gratitude Formula

"Being able to access the inspiration, wit and wisdom of Cathy Jean Norman in the form of a book written with Noelle Nelson is a dream come true. Keep *Sermon on the Molehill* with you and it will surely become the spiritual friend and companion you will turn to time and again."

—**Kim Weiss,**
author, *Sunrise, Sunset: 52 Weeks of Awe & Gratitude*

"I love *Sermon on a Molehill* because Rev. Cathy Jean Norman's 'easy reading' story-telling style teaches Life Lessons in such meaningful and often humorous ways. I found myself thinking/ saying 'Oh yes - I can relate to this,' often! I can't wait to share its messages with my family and many others in my life. Thanks to Rev. Cathy and Noelle Nelson, for this beautiful work, which will truly enlighten and uplift many. It certainly brought me a closer understanding of 'me' and the Higher Power, in my life."

—**Susanne Lammot MD,**
Emeritus Board Member and Past President of the
Boys & Girls Club of Greater Ventura

SERMON ON THE MOLEHILL

Spiritual Keys to Amazing Health,
Wealth and Loving Relationships

BY

CATHY JEAN NORMAN

AND

NOELLE C. NELSON

ISBN: 9781074877781

Media inquiries and contact:
Diane Rumbaugh
Rumbaugh Public Relations
diane@rumbaughpr.com
Cover art by Jason Ray
Formatting by Damonza.com

ACKNOWLEDGEMENTS

I have indeed been fortunate to be surrounded by people who have made my life fuller, richer and sweeter and to whom I wish to express my gratitude. These are the backbone of support that has made this book and other dreams possible.

To my husband and best friend, Steve Blain, the love of my life and a gift from God who makes me laugh every day. Thank you for your love and your constant support and encouragement to be my very best self! I am eternally grateful.

To my Mom, Nancy Norman, my guardian angel. Thank you for teaching me the real wealth of Spirit and for your consistent encouragement. You have always believed in me, for which I thank you. You have blessed my life beyond measure.

To my precious, treasured and beloved lifelong friends and family who have never failed to walk with me over the years: the Jagiellos, Linda Elkins, Bill Shields, Michelle Parent and Skip Smith, Susan Guthrie, the Luckenbacks, the Knechts, Judy

Reimers, the Delongs, The Magnificent 7, Elizabeth Scarbrough and Wendell Liljedahl, Howard Geer, Kim Weiss, Nancy DeCandia and Beth Ann Suggs, Stefani and Natalie Blain, the Heald Family, the Danieles and my dear nephew, Charlie Norman. Knowing each of you has enriched my life with great fun, love, laughter and joy. I am endlessly grateful! May every blessing you have shown me, be upon you and all that you do.

To Unity of Ventura, and all the Unity churches I have been blessed to serve, thank you for letting me teach you these principles that I love so very much - and for always laughing at my jokes. Thank you for your love and loyalty through the years we spent together.

To my treasured co-author, Noelle Nelson, who always gives 100% and whose idea it was to put this book together; you fanned the flame and the idea became a reality. And I am forever grateful for your countless hours of making beautiful sense out of my stream of consciousness. Thank you for giving so much of your brilliance and for your encouragement, love, friendship and support. You are a treasure and a dear friend.

Most of all, I'd like to thank God. Thank you for the signs that show me the way to a most blessed life. I am most grateful for all the good you have given me and continue to bless me with. I love you with all my heart and soul!

~ Cathy Jean Norman

In working with Rev Cathy's sermons, I was once again blown away by how beautifully she translates spiritual principles and wisdom into practical tools for daily life. I am deeply grateful to her for the privilege and pleasure of working with this extraordinary material. Thank you!

My heartfelt thanks also to all those who helped and supported me during the writing of this book, friends and family, most especially my wonderful friends at Unity Church of Ventura. As always, my profound appreciation goes to Diane Rumbaugh and Michelle Masamitsu, whose patience, sound advice and unflagging good humor are invaluable to me in all my endeavors.

~ Noelle C. Nelson

PREFACE

IN 1975, WHEN I was camping with a youth group, I had an experience of translucent Light during a moment of prayer. The Light washed over me, bringing a sense of magnificent peace, which changed my perception of life. I disconnected from the distractions of negative thought. It was very blissful.

That bliss lasted a good three to four weeks. When I woke up each morning, everything was beautiful and intensely alive and serene. I had a new understanding as to how the Universe worked. During that time, my grandmother took me to a Unity church in Santa Monica. As I listened to the Minister give her lesson, I got a very distinct message; "This is what I am to do!" Yet I was only 15 years old!

Fast forward. With my sights set on getting into Ministerial school, I graduated from High School a year early, went on to college and was accepted into Ministerial school at the age of 21. I was the youngest person in my class. My nick name was "Baby MIT" (Minister in Training). When I graduated at 23, I quickly realized that people were not going to take a young female Minister very seriously. I don't blame them, I looked all of 12 years old! On Sundays, people in the congregation would yawn and stare at me, as in "Yeah, really? What can *you* teach *me*?" I figured that the only way I would be able to teach these Truth Principles that I love so much, would be to follow Jesus' example—who may very well have had a similar challenge—and teach by telling stories. Sure enough, I found that storytelling was the best way to capture the attention of my congregation, and that is what I became known for. Now, 35 years later, I have accumulated stories that transform and heal. Some are real life stories and others are tales that can touch the heart like a restorative tonic.

Throughout my years in the ministry, people who've enjoyed and benefited from my sermons have approached me with; "You should write a book!" Every year, I would sit down and try to write a book—but nothing came. I knew how to write a sermon, but a book?! I didn't have a clue.

Then Dr. Noelle Nelson came into my life. She is a congregant and a friend who has written a number of books. One day she and I went out to lunch and once again I heard; "You know, Rev. Cathy, you should write a book." I sighed. "It's hopeless," I told her, "I've tried. Never gonna happen." But Noelle wouldn't leave it at that. She said, "You know how to write sermons, sermons that move people, wonderful sermons. I know how to write books. Maybe together, we can craft a book out of your sermons." Seeing my woeful expression, she continued; "Give it some thought." Grudgingly, I agreed.

As I drove home, and later meditated and prayed, I realized I'm either going to live these principles or I'm not. Not just the ones that are easy for me, but all of them! I'm forever encouraging people not to hide their light behind a bushel, but to take their blessed talents and express them, that it will benefit themselves and others, as it always does. So I figured I'd better practice what I preach (!), get off my self-doubt and lack of confidence in myself as a writer, and shine whatever light I can beyond the sphere of my congregation, out there into the wide world. With that, I took a deep breath, called Noelle and said "Yes! Let's do it!" She responded with a level of enthusiasm that warmed my heart and let me know I was on the right path. Thus, *Sermon on the Molehill* was born.

This book is designed to be a very practical and yet profound body of work. It is intended for those who seek to claim the riches of life, those who want tangible results from their spiritual quest and who are willing to put into practice the very down to earth techniques described. After all, reading these words is one thing, living them is what can make your life positively miraculous. *Sermon on the Molehill* brings you a treasure trove of illumination and direction, woven through a wealth of stories, thought-provoking quotations, parables and humorous quips.

So let me tell you a story…

A Sufi story tells of a poor but honest jeweler, imprisoned for a crime that he did not commit. The guards took pity on the tearful pleadings of his wife, and allowed her to bring her devout husband a prayer rug. Five times daily he would unroll the rug and pray. Time passed, and one day the jeweler proposed the following to his jailers: "I am a very good jeweler. If you give me some pieces of metal and simple tools, I will make you jewelry that you can sell in the Bazaar. I would have something to fill these idle hours, and you would have some extra money." His jailers agreed, brought him tools and metal which they removed—along with whatever jewelry he'd made—every night. All was well. Then one day, the jeweler disappeared! No tunnel or other means of escape was found. He was just plain gone.

Later, after the real criminal had been arrested, one of the jailers saw the jeweler at the Bazaar. "How did you escape?" he asked. "Ah!" replied the jeweler, "My very clever wife obtained the jail plans from the builder, and wove the blueprints into the prayer rug. As I bent my head to pray each day, I began to see the design of the lock which imprisoned me. From there, with left-over bits of metal and the jewelry-tools, I was able to make a key and escape!"

The chapters that follow are keys that will unlock greater understanding for you toward living a life of peace and well-being. It is as if a door opens from within, which allows you to step into a new and larger experience of your life, one filled with magic and wonder. Bask in this healing elixir, and then take the Truth principles out into your world and make them real in your life.

That's where these principles matter. Not as theory, not as conjecture, but to be lived, here and now. Which is why the book is entitled *Sermon on the Molehill*, in contrast to Jesus' famous "Sermon on the Mount," so often depicted in movies as a huge gathering with Jesus speaking from on high. Yet most of Jesus' teaching, as reflected in the Bible, was one-on-one as he went about healing, or in interaction with small groups. I believe that Jesus was very down to earth and personable with a great sense of humor. Throughout my ministry, it has been my objective to reach people at the same level. To be authentic and to assure them that I am just like them, no better or holier in any way shape or form. Just someone who practices these principles with a passion to teach. Thus from a "molehill," my tongue-in-cheek way of saying "I'm with you!"

As you read these pages, it is my hope that when you wake up each morning, everything is beautiful and intensely alive and serene. Blissful!

~ Cathy Jean Norman

In 2010, in the midst of a trying time in my life, I, who had not attended a Church service since my Catholic childhood—although I certainly had followed a spiritual path—was drawn to Unity. I googled "Unity Churches" and went to the one closest to where I live, Unity of Ventura. I walked in, sat down, listened to Rev. Cathy's sermon, and thought, "I'm home." That feeling has never left. My life has since been enriched and expanded in ways I never knew were possible, for which I am deeply grateful. Working with Rev. Cathy on this book has been an inspiring, profound and joyful experience for me.

May reading it bring you peace and light!

~ Noelle C. Nelson

1.

Gamble Everything for Love

A friend of mine was so impressed by a quote from Rumi, "Gamble everything for love," that he did just that. In the process, he told me that once he gambled everything for love, he lost everything! He lost his judgments, his lack of respect, his fears, his anger, even his low self-esteem. In return, he gained everything. He told me how he now loves his life and the people in it, as well as the person he has become. Most of all, he feels how much God loves him, and that is the greatest gift of all.

Love is powerful. Love is transformative. Even with all the love songs, poems, books, movies when you consider our personal conflicts and frustrations, not to mention the world's wars and woes, we obviously haven't said enough about love.

The capacity for love is who we really are. Love holds immense power that we conceal at terrible expense to the world and to ourselves. It is about time that we take scripture seriously when it states, "God is love," and that "Man is created in the image and likeness of God." Mankind is created in and of love. Love is our true nature, whether we realize it or not.

Despite what most people believe, love is not an emotion. It's a way of being. You can't *try* to love, you *are* love. You are rooted and grounded in the all-ness of love. The chief work of one's life is a "call to remembrance" to one's true nature, love, and to get on with the purpose of life, which is also love.

Now as a word or a concept, love cannot solve anything. The activity of loving, however, can solve everything. And that's what the world needs—a new commitment to the action of loving.

We have been taught to think of love as a commodity, rather than as a Divine process. But to love someone is not to give him or her a commodity. It is simply saluting the person's reality, their true essence. It is a process through which you touch and express your own deeper nature. As you look back upon your life, you will find that the moments that really stand out, the moments when you felt most alive, the moments that changed your life, are the moments when you acted in the Spirit of Love.

The experience is never exactly the same, yet at one time or another we have all had experiences of love that have completely transformed our lives. A while ago, I was dealing with a number of very unpleasant situations. I could not feel God's presence. At the time, I was attending a workshop. I was in my "stuff." You know how it goes. I was judging anything and everything. I did not have a whole lot of faith in God at that moment. Although my daily affirmation is, "I ask you God, for a higher awareness of your presence, love and of your guidance," and I said my affirmation diligently, nothing happened. No presence, no love, no guidance.

Well, I was seated at the back of the workshop, still in my "stuff," when all of the sudden I noticed a woman who'd been so moved by something the seminar leader said, that she was crying. A man with multiple sclerosis summoned all of his meagre forces and managed his way painfully across the room to give her a tissue. He went to the woman with such reverence and love in his heart, it was as if he was serving the Lord Himself.

And then it hit me, "God, I see you. I see you, God." I looked around the room, and I could see God in every face. I continued to say, "God, I see you. I see you, God." In that moment, I was transformed by love.

Soon after the workshop, I had the opportunity to stay in that loving place, which as you know, is not always easy out there in the world. I met a woman who let me know that she did not care for me. I looked at her in my heart, and I was able to say to her within myself, "I see you, God. God, I see you."

We all have people in our lives who just aren't on the same page as ourselves. Or perhaps they have hurt us so badly that it is hard to get to that loving place within. Sometimes we have people in our lives that make us think, "All I want is a little revenge! Is that so wrong?"

Here's a simple process to help you get to that loving place even with such individuals.

Bring to mind those people with whom you have an issue. It could be a little issue or a big issue, it doesn't matter which.

Close your eyes for a moment. Now think of a person you totally love and adore. You have so much love for them you can hardly stand it. Imagine putting your arms around this beloved person, and giving them as much love as you possibly can. Put every ounce of your being into it.

Now switch the loved person for the person with whom you have an issue. Give them the same kind of love.

Take a deep breath, and open your eyes.

A Course in Miracles states, "The holiest place on earth is where an ancient hatred has become a present love."

You have all the love you need to heal the relationships in your life that need healing. You have all the love you need for you to enjoy happy human relationships right there within yourself. Those who bitterly declare that their lives are without love are looking to find it outside of themselves. People spend years trying to find love. But love is not to be found. Another person is not the source of your love. You are.

True love is an inside job! Realize that love is within you, and that you can release this love into the world and to others through your thoughts, words, feelings and actions. Then you will no longer feel at the mercy of other people, situations or conditions. You will become master of your world, free from hurt and disappointment.

As a Minister, I have the opportunity to see incredible healing take place through love. Once, there was a woman who despised her father. To her, he was evil. She had not talked to or seen him in 10 years. Her life lacked meaning or purpose, and she realized it was because of the hatred she bore toward her dad. So she decided to send him love everyday. At first, it was very hard to do, but she did it anyway. This went on for almost a year, and then one day he called her and wanted to see her.

I had the opportunity to witness their first meeting. What a tremendous moment! Her dad let her know how proud he was of her, and how much he loved her. Their hearts were wide open and a magnificent healing occurred. They now keep in touch and her life is rich with meaning and purpose.

Her experience is a perfect example of Jesus' injunction to "Love your enemies and pray for those who persecute you." [Matthew 5:43 NIV] A great idea, but not always an easy one to put into practice! However, we can do it because we have access to the center of love within ourselves. No matter how difficult or hopeless your situation may be, when you face it through love, there is always a way out. I have seen relationships heal, businesses flourish, bodies loved back to health and wholeness. Love is the key to life; all of life is for loving.

Become a radiating center of Divine Love and you will find that love changes your whole world!

2.

Prayer Works

September 11, 2001 will go down in history as a day that the Spirit of our nation was not and could not be brought down.

Since then, there have been many other events that severely impacted our communities, and unfortunately may continue to do so—mass shootings, bombings and other such horrors. Even as we come together in our grief at those times, we must also come together in our belief in God.

For even though we may experience anger, rage, sadness, resentment, fear and numbing anxiety, as legitimate and normal as those feelings are, it is not okay for us to stay there. It is not okay to act out those feelings in our own lives. As we go about our individual lives, we cannot become the evil that we disapprove of.

The perpetrators of such hideous events want us to stay in

fear and rage, to stoop to their level. Each of us must rise to a higher level of consciousness than that of the perpetrators. We must repel evil with good. Replace the negative with the positive. Saturate hate with love. And we do this through prayer. As we join in prayer, we are more united than ever before. We are stronger than ever before—as a Church, as a community, as a nation. It's something that perpetrators of violence do not count on.

When bad things happen to good people it is natural to ask, "Why did God let this happen?" I wish I had the answer to that question. I don't. But my belief is that these heinous events are not a God-job. They are a human job. It will not serve us to blame God at this time. Perpetrators would be only too happy to shift the responsability for their acts onto a supposedly uncaring or unloving God. Do not go to that level. Keep the faith for those who cannot seem to find their faith in these dire moments.

In such circumstances, people have sometimes come to me and ask, "It is always darkest before the dawn, isn't it?" I really had to think about that question. Upon reflection, I realized that everything incubates in the darkness. Whenever new life grows and emerges, darkness is crucial to the process. Whether it is a caterpillar in a cocoon, a seed in the ground or a child in the womb, there is always a time of waiting in the dark—what I think of as "holy dark."

We may find ourselves in the holy dark at times, but let us remember that the most significant events that took place in Jesus' life took place in darkness—his birth, his arrest, his death, his resurrection. You see, even though we feel uncomfortable, afraid, even terrified in the darkness, it often yields extraordinary events.

What extraordinary event could possibly occur as a result of hideous circumstances? Thomas Merton, religious writer, theologian and mystic, said that the darkness can strip away of all of our false selves and make us the persons that we are meant to be. People who are kind and considerate, people who will not gossip but will empathize, people who will not judge but will understand, people who are willing to go the extra mile and serve one another.

Many of us panic in the dark, but all we need to understand is that we're in a holy darkness, through which God invites us to go beyond where we are—beyond our fear, our anger, our resentment, our sadness, our judgments. It's an opportunity for transformation, which will allow us to dispel the darkness and walk back into the Light.

How do we do this? Through the power of prayer. Prayer is the most highly effective spiritual act one can perform. When we pray, we ask for the intervention of Spirit on our behalf, or on the behalf of someone else. If you are watching TV or listening to the news, and you see or hear something that is disturbing—send that person or situation the Light by quickly saying a prayer. If someone in your own world is disturbing you, say a prayer for them. Stand firm in the face of whatever adversity is before you. Keep the high watch, do not give your power away.

When you pray, you deny that there is power in evil simply by aligning your loyalty with God. Those who stand with God never stand alone, while those who take a stand for evil have nothing to stand with them and nothing in Truth to support them. Prayer works.

Some time ago, I heard a news interview with a woman who had been in a terrible car accident. She described how she felt herself being lifted out of her body, and found herself hovering over the accident. She could see the police and the ambulance. She could see the traffic backed up for miles. She could feel and hear the distress and irritability of all the people in that traffic. It felt terrible.

But the woman could also see a beam of light coming toward her. It came from a lady stopped in her car along with everyone else, who was praying for her. She could hear the prayer, so she tuned into it, and that prayer is what kept her at peace. The women then felt her body travel back into her body, and as she was coming back down, she took a moment to remember the lady's license plate.

A month later after her recovery, she asked a friend of hers who worked in the police department to please look up the address of the owner of the car whose license plate she'd remembered. Much to the lady's surprise, the woman who had been in the accident presented her with flowers and thanked her for her kindness, for the peace it granted her in those awful moments where she was suffering terribly, sure she was dying.

Your prayers make a huge difference. When you pray, you access a potent spiritual vibration that can be released in no other way. So whenever a report of war, conflict, death or any other unhappy situation—large or small, personal or global— comes to your attention, meet it silently by taking an inner stand. Go to that higher level of consciousness from which healing can take place.

Prayer works. Pray.

3.

To Thine Own Self Be True

Telling the truth about ourselves is critical to our spiritual growth and yet, such honesty can be downright scary.

A Russian folk story tells of an old crazy-looking woman by the name of Baba Yaga who lives deep in the forest. Baba Yaga has a big pot she keeps at a boil over the fire, that she stirs and stirs. Now Baba Yaga knows all things about everything. She can see right into your soul. If you want her knowledge, you must go into the forest and seek her out. You must be brave, because she is frightening. Baba Yaga requires that you go into dark places within yourself and ask dangerous questions. That you step outside the world of masks, logic and form, into your Truth.

A young seeker comes along, and knocks, terrified, at the door of Baba Yaga's house. Baba Yaga demands, "Are you on your own? Or are you sent here by another?" The young man steps back, still shaking he says, "I am sent by my father." Baba Yaga throws him into her pot and stirs him up!

The next one to attempt the quest is a young woman, who quakes in her shoes as she knocks on the door. Baba Yaga opens the door, and asks, "What are you here for? Are you here for yourself or have you been sent by another?" The young woman replies, "Well, I am here on my own, well, um, because I have to, uh…" She wasn't being authentic. She was just trying to make up reasons and Baba Yaga could sense this, so Baba Yaga threw her into the pot!

Another woman came along, who had traveled far to see Baba Yaga. Baba Yaga confronted her, "Are you here for yourself or are you here for another?" The woman answered truthfully, "Well, to be absolutely honest, in large part I am here for myself. And in large part I come because of others, and in large part I come because you are here, and because of the forest, and maybe because of something that I have forgotten, and for a large part I have no idea why I am here." Baba Yaga exclaimed, "Ah! Come in! You'll do!" The woman's willingness to speak authentically— to speak her Truth as confused as it was—is what allowed her in.

Truth. In a wide variety of situations, to all sorts of audiences, Jesus stresses the importance of what he's about to say with the identifying phrase, "I tell you the truth." This phrase, which Jesus repeats repeatedly, is what Biblical scholars have identified as one of his favorite verbal traits. It was almost as if Jesus couldn't tell a parable or start a story without saying, "I tell you the truth." "I tell you the truth" was, in fact, the essence of Jesus' mission. As he said, "Know the truth and the truth will set you free."

But being willing to know the truth and speak it, is not for the feeble or halfhearted truth student. Put another way, are you ready to be disturbed? Because that's what happens when you seek truth. You will inevitably be disturbed. The Gospel of Thomas states [John 16:12-13], "Those who seek should not stop seeking until they find. When they find, they will be disturbed. When they are disturbed, they will marvel and they will reign over all."

Are you ready to be disturbed so that you can marvel and reign over your consciousness? For it is in your most disturbing moments that you are closer to the truth that can set you free. If you take this lesson in, you will open to greater levels of self-esteem and worthiness. You will connect to your Higher Self. You will have more success and greater joy.

Spiritual growth involves a degree of openness and honesty that most people are not willing to entertain. It requires that we be authentic and look at what is going on inside of ourselves. It requires courage to go into the scary places and ask, "What am I trying to hide?" Only as we live a life grounded in impeccable integrity and authenticity will our daily actions be consistent with our vision for our absolute best life. Impeccable integrity is the foundation of a successful and joy-filled life.

The word "integrity" comes from the Latin word "integer," meaning whole or complete. When you are out of integrity, you may not feel whole. In fact you probably feel "less than." When you live inside your personal integrity and authenticity, you are connected to your core and you can trust yourself.

Now, impeccability comes from the Latin word "peca-tus," which means sin, and the prefix "im" means without. So impeccability means "without sin." In Unity, sin means "self inflicted nonsense" (S.I.N.)—anything you do that goes against yourself. Whatever you feel or say or believe that goes against your true self is Self-Inflicted Nonsense—sin!

For example, if you say one thing to yourself or to another, and then do the opposite of what you are saying, you are not true to your word. You are going against yourself. If you do something that you know in your heart was not exactly honest and make no attempt to clean it up, you are going against yourself. If you settle for less than what you are worth, failing to claim your own value, you are going against yourself. If you support another in living from their weakness and not their strength, or ask others to support you in your weakness rather than your strength, you are going against yourself.

If you blame others for things that you could take personal responsibility for, you are going against yourself. If you do not communicate honestly and withhold your Truth, you are going against yourself. If you have to be right no matter what the cost might be, you are going against yourself. Whenever you go against your true essence, the Truth of your Higher Self, then you are going against yourself. You are indulging in "Self Inflicted Nonsense,"—sin.

As Shakespeare wrote, "And this above all, to thine own self be true. And it must follow as night the day, thou canst not be false to any man." (Hamlet, Act 1, S 3) Now I am going to change that a bit to, "To thine own Higher Self be true." One could make the argument that eating an entire quart of ice-cream is being true to one's self, but it isn't being true to what your Higher Self knows is in your best interest.

It takes tremendous courage to be true to your Higher Self, but without it, it is virtually impossible to progress along the spiritual path. Jesus' most quoted teaching is: "Love thy neighbor as thyself." We usually interpret this teaching to mean that we should be as kind to our neighbor as we would like them to be to us. This is surely true. But there is another meaning to this great teaching—it reminds us to be in integrity with ourselves.

There comes a moment in every person's life when we must choose a different direction, a new path. It is as if there is a fork in the road, and the person standing at the juncture realizes that it is no longer possible to straddle two paths. One path calls to us, "Come over here! It is not the right path for you, but we can go into denial. Come on, it will be fun! Come on, it is more comfortable." But that path is riddled with illusion. It is a path with absolutely no self-care or self-loving in place, no boundaries, yet it would have you think that you are taken care of. It is a path that would have you make decisions and excuses that are not for your highest good, or the highest good of those around you.

The other path is not loud or showy. The other path simply says, "To thine own Higher Self be true." It is the path of self-care and self-love. It is not the most comfortable or easy path at times, but it is always the path that will lead you to your best life.

Jesus articulated this concept very well in the parable of the Prodigal Son. A father gave each of his two sons their inheritance. The younger son was enticed into the far country by the path of illusion. He was deluded into thinking that the way to find himself was through extravagant living. In fact, the word "prodigal," according to Webster's dictionary, means "extravagant to the point of recklessness." The Prodigal Son represents that part of us that is ego-centered, where secrets are covered up, blame is projected, conflict is avoided, lies are told and agendas are hidden.

In time, the Prodigal Son is stripped of his self-worth, purpose and meaning in life. He feels cut off from any connection with Spirit. He is then reduced to feeding hogs for a living, which symbolizes life with a lack of direction and total confusion of values. We've all gone through a Prodigal stage at some time in our lives, in one form or another. Yet, as spiritual beings, it just doesn't pay to sell out our highest selves for a feel-good moment or ill-gotten gain.

The parable continues with, "He came to himself!" This is a crucial turning point. You see, at some point we start to wonder if there might be another way— a better way, a higher way—and there always is. The Prodigal Son realizes that his problem was self-induced. He had chosen the path of illusion, one that was not for his highest good. He had chosen a path where there was absolutely no self-care, and surrounded himself with people who kept him down. It was only when "He came to himself," that he chose the path of "To thine own Higher Self be true."

The Prodigal Son decided to go home. He rehearsed a speech for his father, "Father, I have sinned against heaven and before you. I am no longer worthy to be called your son. Treat me as one of your hired servants." However, before he was able to say anything, his father had arranged a festive homecoming party for him. When you take the path of "To thine own Higher Self be true," the Universe (as represented by the father) lines up in your favor. So the Prodigal Son was given new shoes, which represents the new understanding he had acquired when he made the choice to be true to his Higher Self. He was given rings for his fingers, and the best robe, representing a new self-image of worthiness and a feeling of wholeness—the shift in consciousness that occurred when he began treating himself with the kindness and respect he deserved.

There is much more to be gained from this parable, but for now, let's conclude with the following:

You are born of God and nothing less suits you.

God does not ask you to sacrifice your well-being for that of another.

Someone else cannot truly gain if in the process, you are losing.

When you remain true to integrity, you align with the force of all good.

Know the truth and the truth will set you free.

4.

Be Up-Hearted

There's a gift we all possess that we too often forget about. It comes in the form of sizzle and enthusiasm.

Regardless of the conflicts, crises and disasters going on in the world at any given time, a part of us wants to sizzle with excitement and enthusiasm for life. We want more vitality, liveliness and vigor! But sometimes we are stuck in the muck and mire of negative thinking and all we create is more negativity.

The quality of our experiences in life is determined, first and foremost, by our attitudes. One of my favorite quotes from Ronnie Shakes is, "I was going to buy Norman Vincent Peale's book, *The Power Of Positive Thinking*, but then I thought, what good is that going to do?" Really?!

Don't underestimate the power of your attitude—good or bad. Given that that attitude is what determines the quality of our experiences in life, maybe we should look at the qualities of excitement and enthusiasm.

Let's start with looking at the opposite of those qualities— lethargy or sluggish indifference. This is a condition in which a person is unable or undisciplined to be active physically, mentally or emotionally. I think we have all, at one time or another, felt "sluggish indifference."

Take, for example, a time when you awakened and it was a beautiful morning, but you did not experience it. You were indifferent to the world around you. Someone said to you, "Ah! Isn't it a beautiful day?" You gave them "The Look" and thought to yourself, "Yeah, right." You were non-responsive. Well, you had a response, but you did not respond to the immediate experience of your life.

Contrast your indifferent response with the attitude of our co-founder of Unity, Charles Fillmore, a skinny little 94-year-old man. He would awaken each morning with the exact opposite of a sluggish unresponsiveness to life. He was so caught up with the joy of his life that he would bound out of bed and proclaim, "I fairly sizzle with zeal and enthusiasm as I spring forth with a mighty faith to do the things that ought to be done by me." Imagine that! Ninety-four years old fairly sizzling with zeal and enthusiasm as he sprang forth with a mighty faith to do the things that needed to be done by him.

There are some people not even close to being 94 years old who wake up feeling as if a ton of bricks just hit them. They wake up with the attitude of "Oh man. Another day." Their day starts as a burden instead of a delight. This should be an unacceptable emotional response.

The worst thing that can happen to a miserable person is to have two happy people walk into the room. It is absolutely devastating. It is paralyzing for them. So when we are feeling sorry for ourselves or have a list of all the reasons why our lives have come apart, we surround ourselves with people who will agree with us. We are very careful not to be in the presence of someone who will disagree with our negative attitude.

But here's the thing. As long as our unacceptable emotional responses to life are acceptable to other people around us, we will maintain the attitudes that keep us locked into where we are. Life, however, has a way of not accepting our self-defeating negative attitudes for very long. At some point, life will confront you with a situation that forces you to look and see if maybe there isn't a better way to experience life.

A true story about Norman Vincent Peale shows how life confronted him and how he eventually responded in a more positive way.

When Peale was a young man, he got a job working on board a ship that was going to England. One day the ship hit very high waters, a whopper of a storm where waves were crashing down over the bow of the ship. Everyone on the ship—except for Peale—had been through similar storms and knew that the ship would weather the storm safely.

The captain said to the crewmembers, "I want you to go up on deck and tie everything down." Peale said, "You want me to go up there in this storm? I am much safer lying here on the floor holding on for dear life." Finally, Peale followed the captain's orders and went up on the deck. What did he see, but a crewmember dancing around the deck with the wind and the sea hitting him in the face!

The crewmember was loving every minute of it, but not Peale. He was full of fear. Then, Peale thought, "One person—that crew member over there—is having a good time and I feel like my life is going to end at any moment. What is the difference between him and me? Could my attitude possibly be a choice?" In that split second, Peale realized that everything is about choice. In that moment he decided to change his attitude towards what was happening, to release fear thoughts, be enthused and enjoy himself.

It took Peale a few moments to call forth that inner gift of enthusiasm, but once he did, to his surprise he started to have fun on deck. He slid across the deck and tied off the ropes with enthusiasm rather than dread. Peale chose right then and there to be the master of what was occurring in his life through his attitude towards it.

We all have situations like that in one or another area of our lives. Some of us are hitting high seas right now, paralyzed with fear. Or perhaps we're in sluggish indifference: "That's just the way life is." Whereas another person in the exact situation might have a smile on their face saying, "I know with God I'm going to get through it. So I'll just enjoy the ride." What is the difference? Choice. You can choose to be in fear or sluggish indifference, or you can choose to enjoy the ride. How powerful and blessed your life becomes when you enjoy it!

Your life starts right where you are; you can come alive in spite of circumstances. People who have joy in their lives make a room come alive. I would be willing to bet that time after time in your life, you have been enthralled by people who dared to express themselves with a vitality that extended beyond "same-o, same-o." People who rose so far above their sluggish indifference and their negativity that they dared to excel.

This world and much of what is happening in our current history has been thriving on misery. Happy stories do not sell newspapers or go viral because they lack the titillation of fear and malicious gossip. To be happy, to be enthusiastic about your life in the midst of a world in chaos, or a distressing life situation, feels a little strange doesn't it? Let's face it. Joy and vitality are not the norm, but we yearn for it. Just as we yearn to see people who exude enthusiasm for life.

So if we yearn for others to exude it, why don't you and I become the people who exude it? We know deep down inside that pain and separation are not the way God intended us to live. Proverbs 15:15 states, "A cheerful heart has a continual feast." That's how we need to approach life, as a continual feast of exciting things. Enthusiasm is in all of us. It is what makes life worth living.

When was the last time that you fairly sizzled with zeal and enthusiasm? Let me tell you— you can change any situation for the better with your authentic enthusiasm. Now I did use the word "authentic" advisedly, because authentic enthusiasm is a gift from God, not something manufactured by the ego.

You know the difference. When you're around someone who's trying to be enthusiastic, even jumping all around, but it doesn't feel real, almost obnoxious. That's not authentic enthusiasm. It's the ego playing at it. But you don't have to manufacture joy or zeal. It is a gift from God that already resides within us.

If we have this inner gift and this ability, why do we not let ourselves be turned on by it? Many times, we focus our attention on what turns us off. How many times, have you performed your responsibilities at work with sluggish indifference? As in: "Oh, I have to do that again." Other times, we have predetermined opinions on what it is going to take to make us happy so we can approach life with sizzle.

For example:

"I'll be happy if my spouse finally listens to me"

"I'll be happy if I move to another state"

"I'll be happy if I get a better job"

"I'll be happy if I can live in another house"

Notice that what we think it's going to take to make us happy is always something that hasn't happened yet.

The Dalai Lama once said, "The moment one attempts to seek more happiness is the moment one becomes happy." Seek happiness in what exists in your life right here and now, instead of ignoring what is around you. Because you will find that there are wonderful things going on all the time. One of the things that I love to do is ask each morning, "God, I am living in state of exhilarated contentment. What exciting things do you have in store for me today?" Then I look for them and start seeing some pretty phenomenal things.

When we expect exciting things to occur, we draw to us things that affect us in a positive way. We are only miserable when we declare that we are miserable. As stated in Job 22:28, "You shall decree a thing and it will be established onto you." In this moment, you could be the master of how you experience what is occurring in your life. What are you the master of? Your negativity? Your judgments? Or your excitement and your enthusiasm?

Life is about choice. You can be in negativity and sluggish unresponsiveness, or you can enjoy the ride. How powerful and blessed your life becomes when you enjoy it! Your life starts right where you are, and you can come alive in spite of circumstances. Choose to approach your life with enthusiasm and joy. No matter what you are doing, say to yourself, "I am enjoying this!" and watch what happens.

Dog Theology Versus Cat Theology

"Dog Theology" goes like this: "You feed me. You pet me. You shelter me. You love me. You must be God!" "Cat Theology" goes like this: "You feed me. You pet me. You shelter me. You love me. I must be God."

Actually, humans are a mixture of both. We have the ability to tune into God, in and around us, everywhere present. When you're tuned into the frequency of God, the Universe is free to line things up for you, work things out and magical things happen. Instead of staying on that clear, sweet channel where magic happens, most of us hit a bump in the road and immediately start stressing, worrying and fretting. In other words, we create static that blocks the magic always working in our favor from coming through.

Okay, so here the deal. Just take a moment, right now, to tune into the frequency of God within you. Take a deep breath in, and just *know* that your whole day is lining up with magical surprises and serendipitous happenings.

What a great way to start your day!

5.

Soul Transcendence

Recently, I had one of those weeks where unexpected things came up that needed to be handled. And there were times this week when I was most definitely in discord. Meaning out of accord, out of connection with Spirit, with all that is good.

When you're in discord, there is something physically, mentally or emotionally that is out of place. Think of an area in your life where you usually go into discord—family, finances, work—or all of the above!

Now, what's interesting is that discord is not your enemy, but rather a friend in disguise. Discord will tell you where you are giving your power away. Discord will tell you what you need to look at. Discord is giving you the opportunity to change something that is no longer working in your favor. When you resist listening to your discord, it will grow in intensity. Discord will not be ignored. It ferments, growing ever more intense, until it is handled. So discord is something to pay attention to.

A prime example of discord is what happened at that first Easter. After the Resurrection, the Disciples were tried and tested for some of the most terrible things that you could be tried and tested for—grave robbing, slander, insults, telling the truth and just for knowing Jesus. During this time, the Disciples isolated themselves. They no longer felt like they belonged. They were in discord.

Bear in mind that the stories in the Bible are also stories about you and me. Haven't you at times isolated yourself and felt like you didn't belong? Blamed the outside world, other people, lived in fear and righteousness? That's exactly how the Disciples reacted in their woundedness and hurt. Who could blame them? But what we teach here at Unity is that everything is an inside job. How we are in the world depends on our inner world.

At that point, Divine Intelligence stepped in and the Disciples' Higher Selves told them to go to the Upper Room to pray, a very symbolic act. Meaning, they had to remove themselves from the lower level of consciousness that they were entertaining, and rise to a higher level. As the story goes, when the Disciples were in the Upper Room a great wind—the Holy Spirit—filled the room. It cleansed them, purified them, washed over them, and they went into a state of pure elation.

You see, something very interesting happened here. The Disciples came into one accord with God, Universal Power, Spirit. They came into one accord with each other and with their Higher Selves. They were completely connected with a power greater than their "little selves," their ego selves: one chord, one Harmony, one note, one sound, one Beingness. In that one accord, they had to put aside their righteousness, their indignation, their anger, their blame, their judgments, their problems, their own inadequacies, their own insecurities. They had to take all of their false beliefs and let them go, as if to say, "Today, right here and right now, I don't have these beliefs. I only have one thing and that is being in one accord with God." They were in pure enlightenment!

One accord. One connection! That is soul transcendence. Call it what you will. Being connected to the Christ, Nirvana, Shangri-La, Bliss, Heaven, the great beyond, Universal love, a place where suffering (or cellulite!) does not exist. If you are not in one accord with God, if you are not feeling connected to Spirit, yourself, and to your fellow brothers and sisters, it is because you believe in two powers instead of one. You have given false beliefs, like righteousness, accusations, anger, resentment, and fear a warm bed, good food and a comfortable home in the realm of your thoughts, awareness and attention. It is those very beliefs that isolate you from others and the world you live in.

As Dr. Brene Brown states in her book, *The Gifts of Imperfection*, "We are wired for connection. It is in our biology. From the time we were born, we need connection to thrive emotionally, spiritually and intellectually. The connectedness we experience impacts the way our brain develops and performs. Therefore our innate need for connection makes the consequences of disconnection much more real and dangerous."

You and I are hard wired for connection with God and with each other. In order to connect, we must rise to the Upper

Room in consciousness. As we saw with the Disciples, if you are in the lower room of gripping, whining and complaining, you isolate yourself. You are no longer connected—a very sad and lonely place to be.

Connected. Think about that word for a moment. What does it mean to be connected? First, it means power. When we hear someone say, "I have connections," it means, "I have access to power, wealth. I can get it done." Being in the Upper Room in consciousness means that you are connected to Spirit, that you draw to yourself people and opportunities that resonate with that higher vibrational frequency. It means that you are connected to everything you need.

So from there comes the next question: how are you connected to someone who is well-connected?

Some years ago, a woman came into my office. She needed $10,000 to get her business started. She'd designed a service to help women who were newly divorced or widowed, or women who simply needed to get out of an unfortunate situation, to start over. However, she didn't know how she was going to get her start-up money. The bank had turned her down and she didn't know anyone who had $10,000.

The woman became disconnected. She was living in a lower level of consciousness, filled with fear, disillusionment and doubt. Her ego-self wanted to give up. We talked about the idea of getting well-connected to a Higher Source. Together we went into the Upper Room, and there we connected to a Higher Vision, rather than the disillusionment and doubt that the woman was experiencing. You see, in the Upper Room all possibility exists, for it is there that Spirit has infinite supply. In the realm of God, all things are possible!

The woman practiced the feeling that the $10,000 was somehow going to be supplied, and that being well-connected to Spirit—who certainly can supply well over $10,000—was going to connect her to someone, or some idea, or some situation, that could help her. She didn't know how, she just lived "as if" it had already happened. She trusted that all things were going to line up for her good. Every day, she made it a ritual to see and feel herself receiving the money and enjoying a great, successful business. She was living from Upper Room consciousness. She was in one accord with all possibility.

Within a few months, the woman received a call from someone she didn't know in Australia who had heard about her business endeavor through a friend of a friend of a friend. That person wanted to invest $10,000 in her idea—all the way from Australia! If you are well connected to Spirit, you will be connected to the right people and situations at the right time, no matter where they are on the planet. You are open to a Power that makes extraordinary things happen, and not just in matters of financial abundance.

For example, a good friend of mine wanted a lifetime partner. He went into one accord with Spirit. He went into the Upper Room in consciousness, and every day lived in the realm of possibility. One day he went to the airport to pick up a friend, and lo and behold, there he met an English lady who was to become his lifetime partner. They married and now live in England having the time of their lives. When you are well connected, there is absolutely no limit to the number of positive things that can happen!

Here is a process that will help you get and stay well connected in the Upper Room of consciousness to manifest your best life:

Close your eyes and imagine that you are entering into a house.

You are entering the lower level.

Notice where you get hung up in resistance—leave all that behind. Remember, the Disciples let go of their fears, doubts and judgments by saying, "I only have one thing and that is being in one accord with God."

Now go up the stairs into a higher level of the house—the Upper Room of your consciousness.

Highly well connected people think from the end, experiencing what they wish before it shows up. Imagine what it is you desire, in your mind's eye, live it, taste it, enjoy it and be one with it. When you do this, you are making your miracle very real.

The ego self will want to see "how" your desire will manifest. Focus on the "what," not the "how" or the "when." You don't need to know how, that is Spirit's job!

Lastly, be open to all possibilities. When you are open to all possibilities, you are allowing Spirit to express in ways that are much greater than any way you might have imagined. Affirm: "I entrust the good desires of my heart to God's loving care, for I know that with God all things are possible."

For they are! And so it is, amen.

6.

Out of the Cocoon

Once upon a time, there was a young princess who met up with a magic genie. The genie told her he could grant her three wishes.

"Well, okay. I want to be the most beautiful woman in the world!"

POOF! She became the most beautiful woman in the world.

"For my second wish, um—I would like the homiest and the coziest house right in the middle of a plush forest!"

POOF! The most inviting house appeared in a plush forest.

Meanwhile, her dog was barking and barking, so the princess said, "And now please turn my dog—my best friend—into the most handsome prince ever, mine forever more."

POOF! The dog turns into the most handsome prince around.

The prince looks at the princess and says, "I bet you wish you hadn't had me neutered."

When change comes, we are sometimes not quite ready for it. One moment you could be at peace with your world, and the next moment you're struck by major change. Perhaps you lost a job or broke up with a loved one. Or perhaps some special plan for your future has been derailed. Maybe you are thinking of making some changes on your own—like moving, or going back to school, or selling a business.

Not long ago, a newspaper reporter interviewed a tightrope walker at a circus. The reporter shouted up, "How does it feel up there?" The performer looked down at him and said, "I feel suspended firmly in midair." That phrase stuck in my mind. There have been a number of times when I felt suspended in midair, suspended between two worlds—the world I left and can't go back to and the world I want to reach.

Most of us will face changes at some point in our lives that seem to come from left field. Just when we think all is well, our lives change in a very dramatic way. We are suspended in midair between the world as we knew it and the world that will result from the change we've been handed. Truly, the only permanent thing in life is change.

You and I experience more changes in a course of a year than our ancestors experienced in a lifetime. Change, my friends, is not optional. Despite that, very few people like change because the greatest of all human fears is the fear of the unknown. Change propels us into new territory where old maps or old ideas no longer serve us. How we react and what happens inwardly during change, determines our future—whether we fall off the wire or make it safely to a better place.

Some of the not-so-helpful ways we humans tend to react to change are:

Withdrawal—Sometimes we withdraw in defeat. We hide, curl up, get into bed and won't venture out.

Anger—We become embittered and resentful, wanting to strike back and hurt those who have hurt us.

Depression—Another reaction is to go inward and turn anger toward ourselves. We feel rotten inside and say things like, "The future looks grim. This new change will never work."

Substance abuse—We turn to food, alcohol or drugs to numb the pain, trading one problem for another.

While these reactions are all too human, they are the very thing that cause us to lose our balance and topple off the wire. It's the fearful side of us that looks desperately for something outside of ourselves to hold onto. But the only way to stay firmly in midair is to look toward the God within ourselves.

Here are some ways to use the strength of God to stay centered and balanced:

1. Stay focused on what you want, not what has happened.

Focus tightly on what you are trying to do in life, recognizing what you still have, not on what you've lost. A friend of mine got divorced 10 years ago. If you were to talk to her today, you would think she just got divorced yesterday. Her focus is still on the past. Her focus is on what she thinks she lost, definitely not toward the betterment of her future. She has been suspended in midair for a very long time.

So stay focused on what you want, not what has happened.

2. Maintain your inner spiritual poise.

Do whatever works for you to keep yourself centered in a place of spiritual calm and poise. We are all different in this realm. Some people stay centered and poised best when they are alone. Others find this sense of balance when they are outdoors with nature. For some, meditation works. Others of us reach out to those of like Spirit who are closest to us and ask them to hold us in prayer.

I have a few things that I find helpful. I usually talk things over with a friend, do some exercise, and go into quiet time and allow God to purify my being. Find what fits for you and work it!

3. Practice being resilient, then use your resiliency in times of stress.

Sometimes we only know the level of our faith, our belief and our convictions as a result of the challenge we face. Resiliency of Spirit is essential. Rather than being defeated by trouble, you can learn from it, grow, and benefit from it.

One of the spiritual tests we are given is to learn how to become comfortable when we are in midair, rather than be in complete fear and eventually topple off the wire. I share these thoughts with you in hopes that they will help you remain firmly balanced when you are in midair so that when you are between worlds, you can go to God for the strength to get off that wire and get to the world where you want to be.

If you are going through a change in your personal life, think of what a butterfly knows. When the butterfly is but a caterpillar, it begins to spin a cocoon. It doesn't do so because the caterpillar says to itself, "Hey! Today is a nice day—I think I'll spin a cocoon." No. The caterpillar spins its cocoon because it has a Divine impulsion. It simply *must* begin without really knowing what it is doing or what will come next. But what the caterpillar does know is that change is not optional.

Somehow, the caterpillar also knows that the cocoon is not the end result. It must transform into a butterfly. Interestingly enough, when the caterpillar goes into its cocoon, its entire body liquefies. It is either going to go forward or become stuck as a bit of jelly. The caterpillar knows instinctively that the energy it will take to go through the transformation is worth it. What joy to be a butterfly!

It would be wise to keep in mind that the changes we encounter are for the unfoldment and advancement of the soul. Our soul is ready for the change it has been called into, even if we do not feel we are! But through any kind of change we must remember that God is doing a far greater thing than we can see. Just as with the caterpillar spinning its cocoon, you may not be able to see the end result, but God can.

The key to understanding change is to recognize that it is a process, a natural occurrence. Sometimes when you are in the midair of the process it can feel uncomfortable, but it can also be very exciting. It all depends on how we choose to relate to it.

When your life throws change your way—and I guarantee there will be changes—changes you did not plan on, you may find yourself in some very uncomfortable situations. You get to choose whether to shift your point of view from "I can't" to "I must," or from "impossible" to "imperative."

A student went to his teacher and said that he want to be enlightened. His teacher replied, "Go into the hills and meditate for three days." The student went and meditated for three days. After three days he returned and said, "Teacher, I am not enlightened. What shall I do?" The teacher said, "Go meditate for three more days. Then you will achieve enlightenment." After three more days, the student was not enlightened. The student cried, "Teacher, I am still not enlightened! I must not go back to my family without achieving enlightenment."

The teacher furrowed his brow, deep in thought, and replied, "Go back into the hills for three more days. If you do not achieve enlightenment by then, you might as well kill yourself." The student went back up into the hills and on the second day he was enlightened. He very quickly shifted from "impossible" to "imperative," from "I can't" to "I must"!

Change happens! Sometimes, a condition will arise in your life that indicates you need to make a change. You will be pushed and shoved by circumstances and events until you make that change. When that happens, rely on God. Realize that it is not so much that a door has closed on a chapter of your life, rather that a door has opened to more interesting possibilities and opportunities.

Often we like to hang out in our uncomfortableness, to complain, grip, moan and groan. Instead, remember to use your uncomfortableness as a stepping-stone, not a campground. Your uncomfortableness can be a place of profound empowerment, as long as you remember that although everything of this world changes, God is changeless. God is the same yesterday, today and forever.

This great Truth has been known in all religious traditions. No matter what is going on in our lives, God is the same. Teachers, Ministers and children leave, jobs change, people we love pass on, but God never changes. God is always fully present. This unchanging God resides at your very center. This unchanging God has always resided in and as the very essence of you.

That means that you are one with a Power that is changeless. No matter what happens in your life, the central core of you cannot be moved. It is this central core that knows exactly what it is doing, and invariably doing a far greater thing than you can see. Sometimes, we get impatient and we think our way is better than God's natural process. But God has His own timing, and we can rely on Him, for in the midst of what looks like chaos, we are always taken care of. There is a bigger plan that we are not aware of.

Change is the law of the Universe. Without change, the world would remain in a static state and soon become stale and stagnant. Without change there would be no progress, for change is the very essence of all improvement. It is quite obvious that to do anything in a new and better way there must be change.

The Bible does not state, "Cling to the old," it states, "Behold I make all things new." [Revelation 21:5] Embrace change and allow the new into your life!

7.

God's Grace

One night a house caught on fire and a young boy was forced to the roof. His father stood on the ground below with outstretched arms, calling to his son, "Jump! I'll catch you." He knew that his son had to jump in order to save his life. However, all the boy could see between himself and his dad was fire, smoke and darkness. As you could imagine, the boy was filled with panic. His father yelled again, "Jump, son! I will catch you." But the boy protested, "Daddy, I can't see you!" His father replied, "But I can see you and that is all that matters."

If you are in a place where you don't know where to go or what to do next, know that God sees the way and spiritual assistance is available to you all the time. It's called Grace. Sometimes Grace doesn't feel present because we are too caught up in the struggle. Grace happens when you bring yourself into alignment with the divine essence within you, God's ever-present spiritual assistance. When Grace is present, there is harmony within and peace within your life.

Know this about yourself—you have as much of this divine essence available to you as the holiest man or woman. It is yours to accept. That is the key word—accept. Some of you might be saying, "Grace is not here for me. I don't feel that divine essence." But whether you are aware of it or not, take heart. God's Grace, His Divine Essence is here right now and is actively working on your behalf.

A story is told of the only survivor of a shipwreck who washed up on a small, uninhabited island. He prayed feverishly for God to rescue him, and every day he scanned the horizon for help, but none came. Exhausted, the man eventually managed to build a little hut out of driftwood to protect him from the elements and where he could store his few possessions.

Then one day, after being out looking for food, he arrived home to find his little hut in flames, the smoke rolling up to the sky. The worst had happened. Everything was lost. The man, stunned with grief and anger, cried out, "God, how could you do this to me!" He went to sleep that night angry and confused. However, early the next day, he was awakened by the sound of a ship approaching the island. It had come to rescue him! "How did you know I was here?" asked the weary man. "We saw your smoke signal," replied the ship's Captain.

It is easy to get discouraged when things go bad. Some of you may be facing difficult situations right now. We should never lose heart because God is at work in our lives even in the midst of pain and suffering. Remember, next time your little hut is burning to the ground, it may be a smoke signal that summons the Divine Essence of God, the Grace of God.

Metaphysics teaches us that the fundamental cause of human suffering are negative thoughts, negative emotions, self-ish motives, unhappy memories, fears, hostility, guilt, anger, envy, resentments, jealousy, holding a grudge and so forth—erroneous beliefs and attitudes.

The problem with negativity is that too often, we have either suppressed it in our minds, buried it in our souls, or we may be deliberately holding on to and continuing to express it. This is the reason one may be suffering in a difficult situation yet cannot figure out why. Modern day psychology confirms that much of negativity or sin is hidden or suppressed on the deeper levels of the subconscious. The buried or hidden nega-tivity is what often translates into mysterious symptoms such as depression, illness or unhappiness in the mind. For example, perhaps when you were young someone—a teacher, a parent, a good friend or even complete stranger—told you or gave you the impression that you weren't "good enough" at something, be it at school work, dancing, basketball or whatever. Until that person said that to you, or made you feel that way, you might not have thought that about yourself, but now that someone else's thought has made its way into your mind, you've accepted it as true.

Unless you had reasons or evidence otherwise to challenge it, you've adopted that other person's belief as your own. Such a belief can be hidden deep in your subconscious, leading you to make negative decisions from an unconscious level. Now, if in order for you or me to be healed we would have to discover each hidden and suppressed error or negativity within ourselves, and treat each one as we discovered to try to get rid of it. We would have to take inventory and deal with each one, face to face—a huge task!

I am a big believer in getting counseling, and certainly using this way of healing can be extremely beneficial. However, it is not the only way to heal, because Grace is available to all of us. Therefore, it is not necessary for us to discover all these suppressed errors or negativity—a good thing, because at least for me, it would take me forever. All we need to do is to admit that there are some suppressed errors and negativity and that we do not want to hold onto them, whatever they may be.

Accepting the divine essence of God, the Grace of God, is what sets each and every one of us free. As this Divine Essence enters your being, a powerful process occurs. Spirit cleanses, forgives and heals us, and everything negative can be swept away completely.

Many of you know exactly what I am talking about. You have experienced Grace or may even be experiencing it now. The Grace of God is such a beautiful thing that it is difficult for us to express it in language. Whether or not we can comprehend the Grace of God with our minds, we know that our hearts can always comprehend Grace when we are experiencing it. Our hearts know the Grace of God instinctively.

We may experience Grace in any number of ways. Sometimes we receive a wonderful blessing of some kind, which we do not think that we really deserve. We may wonder why such a good thing has happened to us. We may wonder if it is just a matter of luck or coincidence. But it may well be that we have simply opened ourselves to the Grace of God, and have attracted to ourselves a blessing that Karma would have never have brought to us. Grace transcends Karma.

For example, last week was a delightful and difficult week for me. It was delightful because my mom came into town for a visit. It was difficult. On Monday when we came to Church to do some work, I found three pieces of correspondence that needed my attention. One letter was from the IRS, another was from my insurance company and another was from the moving company. Let's just say, none of these letters were in my favor.

I panicked. Then my mom said, "Why don't you invite Grace in by giving the Universe a 'to-do' list?" Wise advice! I took out a piece of paper and drew a line down the middle of the page. On one side, I put what I was willing to do and on the other side, I wrote down what the Universe was to do. Within days, Grace came rushing forth. The IRS situation was resolved, the moving company came through and I have no doubt the insurance company will be resolved as well.

Grace transcends Karma in many other ways. People often report having been careless while driving their car and miraculously narrowly escaped from serious traffic accidents. In matters of human relationships, instead of the usual quarrel, the Grace of God establishes greater understanding and forgiveness—all without strenuous effort on your part. When you've been rejected from a job or a relationship, remember that every rejection is God's protection. It is divine intervention—Grace.

A story of Grace I particularly like involves a family friend who was given only six months to live. The doctor sat her down and said, "You have an aggressive form of cancer. It would be wise for you to get your affairs in order at this time." The woman responded by saying, "I am a child of God. And in God there is no illness." The doctor thought she was in shock, so he repeated himself. The woman then repeated herself. After which, she got in her car to go home and the Grace of God washed over her.

Seven years later the woman got the flu. She went to the same doctor. He was shocked!

He was sure that she was long dead. The doctor ran a battery of tests and there was no cancer to be found. That was 20 years ago.

How does one find the Grace of God? How does one connect with it? You know, I wish the answer to that were very complicated and highfalutin so it would make a big impression on you. But, in truth, the answer is very plain and simple. All you need to do is believe in the Grace of God with all your heart and become totally willing for it to become the law of your life. That's all.

Grace is directly under control of the Holy Spirit. It is God's expression of love for His children even His children who make mistakes or who sin. Grace corrects mistakes and forgives sin. God's Grace is for me and for you and for all people everywhere. But we have to open ourselves to it, and we must respond to it, not with questions or demands for explanations, only with willing and thankful hearts.

So when the job disappears, the marriage goes sour, the children act up and the car breaks down, all in one day; when it seems like it is 1,000 degrees outside and your best friend is out of town, and you have to reach far to find something to be happy about. When all of this is going on and you call forth spiritual assistance—if you acknowledge the spirit of Grace to wash over you, I guarantee you will feel a peace beyond all understanding and you will know that this too shall pass.

Be willing for Grace to be the law of your life. When that Divine Essence is extended to you, share that essence with other human beings, not by talking about it, but by being it.

Here is a prayer to help you affirm Grace in your life:

God's Grace is with me right now.

God's Grace is given freely to me right now.

God's Grace is now working on my behalf.

Amen!

8.

Five Kernels of Corn

Every year in the United States we celebrate Thanksgiving. All over America, families and friends gather around the dinner table to rejoice in their bounty of blessings.

However, in many ways, it is one of the craziest weeks of the year. Between the jam-packed freeways and over-crowded airports, the kids who'd rather do anything other than make nice with Uncle Harry or Great-aunt Susan, hours of mindless conversation with relatives you hardly know and whose lives and forcefully voiced opinions are the polar opposite of yours, and then, finally, having to corral everyone for the trip home, stuffed, sluggish and grumpy!

Somehow, in the thick of this, we forget the reason for the holiday. For example, take Jesus' miracle of the loaves and the fishes [Matthew 14:18-20 NIV]: "Bring them here to me," he said. He directed the people to sit down on the grass. Taking the five loaves and the two fish and looking up to heaven, he gave thanks and broke the loaves. Then he gave them to the disciples, and the disciples gave them to the people. They all ate and were satisfied, and the disciples picked up 12 basketfuls of broken pieces that were left over. Or Jesus' miracle of Lazarus rising from the dead [John 11:39-41 NIV], "Take away the stone," he said. "But, Lord," said Martha, the sister of the dead man, "by this time there is a bad odor, for he has been there four days." Then Jesus said, "Did I not tell you that if you believe, you will see the glory of God?" So they took away the stone. Then Jesus looked up and said, "Father, I thank you that you have heard me."

One of the reoccurring themes in these miracles is that Jesus gave thanks *before* the miracles came into manifestation. As he performed each miracle, Jesus would first look to heaven and give thanks. He looked away from the appearance of lack and gave thanks from an elevated consciousness.

If you want miracles in your life, if you want to overcome untoward circumstances in your life, the secret is to give thanks for what you want right in the midst of the circumstance, *before* there is any reason to give thanks.

Why is giving thanks so powerful? Because words that express gratitude release certain potent energies of mind and body that are not otherwise tapped. Gratitude liberates the finer essences of the soul that are necessary to bring about miracles. Gratitude begets Grace.

Grace has been described as the influence or spirit of God in operation, the freely given favor and good will of God. In Unity, we say that Grace is uncontaminated conscious light, uncontaminated meaning without judgments, without over analyzing, having resentment, guilt or always having to be right. Grace is the illumination of Spirit, it is Divinity. Grace is extended to you by the depth of your gratitude. When you are in gratitude, you draw to you and invoke Grace, and Grace is what begets a miracle.

A woman had become a mental and physical wreck by dwelling on her problems. She complained about everything and everyone, her aches and pains and depression, and as she did her woes multiplied, which indeed they would, for whatever you focus on, increases. Finally, the woman went to see a doctor who was very wise. She told him all of her problems, whereupon he asked, "Now that you have told me all that is wrong with you, tell me something that is right with you." The woman protested angrily that there was nothing right with her. The doctor persisted, "There must be something right with you. You are able to walk, talk, see, hear, taste, smell. You are not bedridden or helpless. You are enjoying some degree of health or you would not be here."

The woman finally agreed that there was something right with her health—her little finger was perfect. The doctor told her to go home and for three days, give thanks for the health of that finger. Three days later, the woman came back and her whole hand was without pain. The doctor worked with her in this fashion until her whole body was completely healed. Not only was the woman happy, but she had found meaning and purpose to her life. A miracle? For this woman, it was. Grace was extended to her by the depth of her gratitude.

In certain regions of Mexico, hot springs and cold springs are found side by side. Because of the convenience of this natural phenomenon, the local women often bring their laundry there. They boil their clothes in the hot springs, and then rinse them in the cold springs. A tourist watching this procedure commented to his Mexican guide, "They must think Mother Nature is generous to freely supply such ample, clean, hot and cold water." The guide replied, "No. There is much grumbling because she supplies no soap." Sometimes we complain so much that we forget to see the blessings right in front of us. Find something that you can be grateful for and Grace will be extended to you by the depth of your gratitude.

We are taught from a very young age that being grateful is an important social grace. Indeed, it is but even more, it is essential for a high level wellbeing. It is crucial for being happy, as many great thinkers and philosophers have described.

In *The Power of Giving Thanks*, Jeff Jacoby writes, "Gratitude is nothing less than the key to happiness." Dennis Prager, author of *Happiness is a Serious Problem*, writes, "There is a secret to happiness, and it is gratitude. All happy people are grateful, and ungrateful people cannot be happy. We tend to think that it is being unhappy that leads people to complain, but it is truer to say that it is complaining that leads to people becoming unhappy. Become grateful and you will become a much happier person." Not only that, but as Plato said, "A grateful mind is a great mind which eventually attracts to itself great things."

The simple act of gratitude will stimulate and increase your good. There was a time in my life when it looked like all doors were closing. I was depressed. I complained about it to everyone who would listen. I felt backed into a corner and I didn't know what to do. Then I came across a quote from Catherine Ponder, "You have no idea how much suffering is caused in the life of a person who dwells on the wrong-doings of their life. If they only knew that with thanksgiving, every obstacle can be overcome."

With that, I remembered Jesus' teaching to look away from the apparent lack and give thanks. I had to call forth a miracle. I had no room for anything less in my life. I invited some of my friends over for a Thanksgiving dinner—in April! We gave thanks for all the good in our lives. My friends helped me focus on all the blessings in my life. Within just a few days, all the doors began to open and my joy returned. It was a miracle!

Never underestimate the power of gratitude. When you have an attitude of gratitude, you are cooperating with the Universe. It is like a great magnet that draws to us many blessings and opens the door to our greater good.

As Charles Fillmore, one of the co-founders of Unity, said, "A state of gratitude is the highest state that we can be in as a human being. When you express thanks, gratitude and praise, there is an energy released from the mind and soul which is usually followed by a profound effect, and you become aware in the NOW moment that God is working in your life and that all is good. You can praise a weak body into strength, a fearful heart into peace and trust, shattered nerves into poise and power. It is a powerful insight to live by."

The first winter the Pilgrims endured in America was so bad, that they each could only eat five kernels a day. Yet each day they were to give thanks for those five kernels of corn. Their miracle came the very next spring, when they received help from their Indian friends, which assured a bountiful harvest, thus the tradition of Thanksgiving.

Each day, take a few moments to thoughtfully, mindfully,

be grateful for five things, no matter what else is going on in your life. Your "five kernels of corn," as it were. This simple act of thankfulness will help accelerate miracles all around you. Grace will be extended to you by the depth of your gratitude and you will be able to call forth miracles in your life, your "bountiful harvest."

Who's Talking Inside Your Head?

Lately, I've realized there are two Cathys who live inside my head. I find it helpful to distinguish between them, to recognize which Cathy thinks she is in charge.

First, there's "Blessed Cathy." She, of course, notices how lucky she is, how amazingly awesome life is and how everything always works out for her good. Then there's controlling "Frantic Cathy." Frantic Cathy tends to notice difficulties and challenges, even teensy little challenges like wrinkles or a belief that something is not exactly how she thinks it should be. Frantic Cathy is filled with fear and worry, and life feels darned chaotic!

It's fascinating to watch which Cathy is generating my thoughts. Nowadays, when I notice Frantic Cathy getting noisy, I simply tell her "Bless you and thanks for sharing." And remind her what *A Course in Miracles* promises—that problems are nothing but a wrong perception. That problems literally wither and die when we don't feed them with our attention.

When we look through the eyes of gratitude, awe and wonder, our whole world changes along with our perception. We realize the truth—that we can never be abandoned, that we have everything we need and that the Universe is constantly working on our behalf and for our betterment.

So here's to paying more attention to your Blessed Self!

9.

The 10 Commandments of Money - #1 & #2

Commandment #1:

You shall look to no other source but God as your supply!

Commandment #2:

Thou shall not think that money is evil.

One of Unity's most important principles is a belief in abundance for all, in prosperity. We believe that it is God's will that every individual on the face of this earth should live a healthy, happy and prosperous life.

Prosperity matters to Unity because we want you to live your dreams, love your life and live out of your greatness. When we talk about prosperity in Unity, we mean being healthy in mind, body and Spirit, having loving relationships, being happy and manifesting goodness.

And yes, we are also talking about money. As Mae West famously said, "I've been rich and I've been poor and rich is better!" So true! Maybe you've had a health issue and didn't have the finances to receive quality health treatments. Maybe you've been burnt out and you wanted to go on vacation but didn't have the finances to do so. Maybe you've wanted to start your own business but didn't have the funds. Rich is better, because when you have money you have more choices.

Lately I re-read some classic spiritual books that were written in the late 1800s and the early 1900s, in particular, *The Art of Money Getting* by P.T. Barnum, *The Gospel of Wealth* by Andrew Carnegie, *The Science of Getting Rich* by Wallace Wattles and *Prosperity Through Thought Force* by Bruce MacLelland. Last but not least, *Prosperity's 10 Commandments* by Georgianna Tree West. Even though I had read these books before, I acquired a richer, newer and deeper understanding as I re-visited them.

I couldn't help but notice that each one of them started their books by saying basically the same thing—that they were financially poor and in ill health until they came across this system that changed their lives from poverty to great financial wealth. Each one of them said to follow the described principles and it is guaranteed that your life will turn around!

Each one of them started at their lowest point. They wanted out of their conditions badly enough to commit to a daily practice, which is what each of them did. Commitment demonstrates a powerful intention, an action, to which Spirit then responds. Not only were these authors committed to their practice, they also followed the law of persistence. For many of them, it took six months to a year before their lives completely turned around. If you want more prosperity in your life, ask yourself, would you be willing to undertake a daily practice for at least six months? The success of any spiritual practice requires that you be persistent.

It is said, "quitters never win and winners never quit" as exemplified by the following story.

Two frogs fell into a bucket of milk. Both were paddling, saying, "Oh no! We are not going to make it out of this!" But they kept paddling and paddling, until finally one of them said, "I quit. I can't do this anymore." That frog promptly drowned. The other frog said, "I am not going to quit! I am going to keep on going!" He kept paddling. After a while—a long while—the milk turned into a thick whipping cream that allowed the frog to hop right out.

The frog survived because he obeyed the law of persistence. You've got to keep going. So many people give up just before their great victory. You must be able to persist with anything that is worthwhile to you. If it is not worthwhile to you, then you will probably not commit to it, and thus will not be able to persist.

The next few chapters are devoted to what I call "The 10 Commandments of Money." They are guidelines on how to live a successful and prosperous life, just as the Bible's 10 Commandments are guidelines on how to live a good life.

For centuries, the world, especially the religious world, has had divided and confused attitudes about money. Money and riches have often been condemned as dangerous to one's spiritual growth and unfoldment. In many religious organizations, it has even been taught that money is the root of all evil. And yet, Churches, Synagogues and Temples would not survive without the kind and generous donations from their parishioners.

Like it or not, money is a great concern and a constant anxiety for many, many people. Even mystics and gurus have to pay the bills! So the question is, how can money be both a very important necessity of life, and yet often be considered a handicap to one's spiritual growth? How can money be sinful or evil when no one, not even religious organizations, can get along without it?

I believe that this contradiction may come from what Paul said in the Bible [1 Timothy 6:10], "The love of money is the root of all evil." This is probably one of the most distorted statements in the Bible, because the word that is often left out is "love." The statement becomes, "Money is the root of all evil," which is not what Paul said, nor what is true. For it is not money per se that is evil, but the *love* of money—greed. It means that if you make money your God, then you have a problem! Money in and of itself, is neutral.

"The 10 Commandments of Money" represent 10 attitudes about money, which will magnetize your mind for money without making it your God.

The first two Commandments are the foundation for all those that follow.

The first is:

You shall look to no other source but God as your supply!

Some of you may feel more comfortable with words such as Universal Power, Divine Intelligence or The Field of Infinite Potential, instead of God. It doesn't matter which word you use, whatever you call it, there is a Divine source behind every supply.

The history of poverty in the lives of many individuals can be directly traced to a lack of faith in what I will call "God" as the source of all supply. Often we think our job is our source of money. We may think that when Aunt Sally dies our inheritance will be our source of money. Or that winning the lottery will do it for us. But here's the deal, no person or organization is the source of your supply. Your job, Aunt Sally, or the lottery are important as channels through which Universal Energy— God's good, God's supply— can flow. Therefore, every good and wonderful thing that flows into your life must have its beginning in God.

As Jesus said [Luke 12:32], "It is the Father's good pleasure to give you the kingdom." The will and purpose of God is to deliver the riches and fulfillment of every good thing into your life. Take a moment to think of all the good in your life and declare these words to yourself:

> *Every good thing in my life has its beginning in God*
> *I shall look to no other source but God as my supply!*

The second Commandment is:

> *Thou shall not think that money is evil.*

The thought that money is evil forms a "money rejection complex," a negative attitude about money that actually repels money from you. As Catherine Ponder, author of *The Prosperity Laws of Receiving*, wrote, "Always, when there seems to be a delay or block between you and your money, that block lies within you, and not in some outside circumstance or personality."

Change your inner landscape and your outer landscape will change.

Questions for you to consider:

1. Do you think that money is evil?

2. Do you think that money is dirty?

3. Do you think that money will corrupt yourself or the people around you?

Often people lack prosperity, but they don't know why until they ask themselves these questions. Then they find that deep within them is some facet of the "money rejection complex"— beliefs that somehow money is evil, dirty and will corrupt you, your life or even the people in your life.

When I was in my 20s, I inherited a substantial amount of money. My "money rejection complex" at the time was that my inheritance would corrupt the people around me. Sure enough, people came out of the woodwork to take advantage of my enriched circumstance. That was only the outward manifestation of my inner belief, my money rejection complex. Needless to say, since then I have rooted that thought out. It is no longer part of my consciousness.

If you are having a problem with money, if you lack the prosperity you desire, look at which of your thoughts may be rejecting money so you can root them out. That's the first step in allowing God's great supply, His abundance, into your life.

10.

The 10 Commandments of Money - #3 & #4

Commandment #3:

You shall not speak the word of lack or limitation.

Commandment #4:

You shall make no mental images of lack.

One of the greatest mistakes we human beings make is to define who we are by money. We define ourselves one way if we have plenty of it, or we define ourselves another way if don't have enough. But the wonderful Truth is that you are not your bank balance. You are not the sum total of your debts or how much you have in your purse or wallet. You are a human being.

More than that, you are a spiritual being in an earth suit

having a human experience. First and foremost you are spiritual! Therefore, you cannot define yourself by money. Money is a specifically human creation. It is a total fabrication of our genius. We made it up and we manufacture it.

However, rather than relate to money as a tool that we created and control, we have come to relate to money as if it is a force to be reckoned with. This stuff called money, which has no more inherent power than a tissue, has become the single most controlling force in our lives, in our country, in our government and in our world. Yet money has only the power we assign to it, and we have assigned it immense power.

Human beings have done and will continue to do terrible things in the name of money. They have manipulated and taken advantage of others for it, lied for it, stolen for it. Some people have hoarded it out of greed, or even enslaved themselves to unhappy lives in pursuit of it.

That being said, the healthy way to view money is neither as "good" or "bad," but as "neutral." It is only the perceiver who determines the value that is placed on money. You assign your projections to money. For example, someone who doesn't have much money would put quite a bit of value on a single dollar bill. Someone who has a lot of money wouldn't put as much value on the same bill.

So let's consider money as energy, which brings me to our third Commandment of Money:

You shall not speak the word of lack or limitation.

Did you know that every time you open your mouth, you paint a living picture to others of your present state of consciousness? People who complain, talk about how poor they are, put themselves down, or declare that they are somehow inferior, without realizing it are speaking volumes about their present state of consciousness. For such individuals, I can guarantee life usually does not work in their favor. On the other hand, people who talk about the good in their lives, speak highly of others, declare all the positives in their lives and are grateful, are also speaking volumes about their present state of consciousness. And I can guarantee that their lives work really well for them.

People are attracted to you or repelled by your words more than by anything else, because words carry their own power. Words are a vital part of your electromagnetic field. They put out energy and attract the same type of energy back to you. In Isaiah 55:11 it states, "My word shall not return to me void, but shall accomplish that whereunto it is sent."

Why is that? As we know the Universe, and everything that exists, is in motion. Everything is energy. As Nikola Tesla said, "If you want to find the secrets of the universe, think in terms of energy, frequency and vibration." The spoken word is a vibrating vehicle of energy that can be sensed immediately. The words that you choose to use either raise or lower your vibrational frequency.

How does that relate to money? Money can hear you. Money has "ears." From this moment forward, start thinking of money as a persona, an intuitive entity. Not only that, think of money as being very aware. Money knows what you are saying about it within yourself. Money reacts to what you think about it and what you say about it. Money will not tolerate any critical talk about itself.

Think about it. If someone is talking badly about you, saying that you are evil, dirty and corrupt, you'd feel that energy and you wouldn't want anything to do with that person! So it is with money. Money hears what you think and say about it. If you insult money, money will have nothing to do with you.

Instead, say:

> *"Money is wonderful. I really like money. Money and I have a great relationship. In fact, I love money and money loves me!"*

It is said that Mary Morrissey, best-selling author and speaker, opened her workshops by fanning a handful of hundred dollar bills, much as you would a deck of cards. She'd kiss the bills, hug them and affirmed, "I love money and money loves me!" She did that on purpose to help people get in touch with their "money rejection complex," as well as to show people that she is a magnet for money to come to her with ease and grace.

You see, Morrissey talks money *to* her she doesn't talk money *away* from her. Talk money *to* yourself, not *away* from you! As it states in John 1:14, "And the Word became flesh and made His dwelling among us!" Your word is always becoming flesh, it is always manifesting and making its dwelling within that manifestation. If you talk about lack of money, you will get more lack of money. If you talk about the abundance of money, you will get more abundance of money.

The Modern Mystery School for Advanced Spiritual Training suggests that you delete a number of words from your vocabulary, one of them being the word "expensive," because it implies that something costs more than a person can afford, and generally has a negative emotional charge about money attached to it. The school recommends thinking of whatever you want to purchase—or not—as a matter of *choice*, without complaint or any other negative talk, which simply would affirm lack.

I thought, "What a great idea!" and with that, decided to delete the word "expensive" from my vocabulary. As I did so, I was amazed at how much I use it, especially as we were renovating our home and getting quotes for various projects. That was an eye opener for me! Now instead of saying, "That is ridiculously expensive!" I say, "I think we can choose something more fiscally responsible given our finances." There is no underlying emotional charge for me with that statement.

Watch the words you use. Remember, money can hear you!

The fourth Commandment of Money, related to the third, is:

You shall make no mental images of lack.

Just as the words you use attract or repel things, so too every mind is a magnet. Science teaches us that each of us emits a field of measureable energy with a certain rate of vibration, a frequency. Like vibrations are attracted to your frequency of vibration and dissimilar ones are warded off. Since form (manifestation) follows consciousness (thought), the power of the mind draws certain events, circumstances and people into our lives and repels others. It does this through the law of attraction. Like attracts like.

The story is often told about Jim Carrey, the famous movie actor. When he was broke and poor at the beginning of his career, he deliberately visualized getting calls from producers and directors wanting to hire him. He didn't really know what he was doing with his visualizing, only that it made him feel better. Then one day he decided to write himself a check for $10 million for acting services rendered. He dated it five years ahead—Thanksgiving 1995.

Jim put the check in his wallet where he would see it every day. Just before Thanksgiving 1995, he made $10 million for his work in the movie "Dumb and Dumber." Now Jim didn't just sit back, visualize and eat cookies. He worked hard. We will address the Money Commandment of Action in the next chapter. However, if you can see it and believe it, it is a lot easier to achieve it!

The Universe is perfect, loving and it is always here to serve you. Imagination—what you are thinking and visualizing—is how you work with the Universe. Imagination is what calls forth the likeness of things that you have entertained.

If you are entertaining being poor, the Universe is here to serve you.

If you are entertaining being rich, the Universe is here to serve you.

Your imagination comes with great responsibility. It can charm and bewitch you, it can frighten or enlighten you, it can lift you to ecstasy or plunge you into despair. The world around us tempts us into entertaining images of deficiency and inadequacy. It bombards us with negativity, limitation and lack. It tells us all that we can't do and what we can't become.

Therefore, it is of vital importance that you take time every day to imagine goodness in your life! Keep your thought-frequency, your vibration, in a high and positive place. Be vigilant, so that you make no mental images of lack.

11.

The 10 Commandments of Money - #5 & #6

Commandment #5:
You shall feel Higher Sensations.

Commandment #6:
Thou shall get off thy But/Butt.

Most people have an angst-ridden relationship with money. They think that money is limited, demanding and unstable, that it is out of their control and in the hands of "the economy" or "the government" or "Wall Street." Thoughts like these do not make for a happy relationship with money.

Recently I came across the following quote from the poet Iain Thomas, "Every day the world will drag you by the hand yelling, 'This is important! And this is important! And this is important! You need to worry about! And this! And this!' And each day it is up to you to yank your hand back, put it on your heart and say, 'No. This is what is important.'"

So true! Which is why it's time to lay another foundation about money.

Over the centuries, money has gotten a bad rap because it has been associated with corruption and the misuse of power. A perception has developed that the rich deprive the poor, and that if you became wealthy, you disconnect yourself from love, goodness and all things worthy. This, by the way is a "Money rejection complex" thought, as we discussed in a previous chapter. But here's the thing, poor people can also disconnect from love, goodness and all things worthy!

It's hard to align with money if you think money is evil or corrupt in some way, or if you think rich people are evil and corrupt.

You need to be aware of how subtle these money rejection complexes are and catch them before they take you down the rabbit hole of negativity, thus blocking money from coming into your life. Once you come into alignment with the idea that money is neutral, you can see that it can be used in well-intended ways, with kindness and generosity. I sincerely believe that you can be rich and spiritual, and that with your abundance you can create a lot of goodness in the world.

The Bible is full of statements about prosperity:

John 3:2: "Beloved, I wish above all things that you shall prosper."

Deuteronomy 8:18: "But remember the Lord your God, for it is He who gives you the ability to produce great wealth."

Often, when Jack Canfield, co-author of the wildly successful *Chicken Soup for The Soul* series, was interviewed about how he got started, he'd tell the following story, the gist of which is as follows. Canfield was studying the works of W. Clement Stone, who stated, "You should set a goal that's so big, and so unbelievable, that if you achieved it, you'd know it was a result of following this program for success. And to stay in the question, *'What would you do if you just knew it wasn't impossible?'*"

So Canfield decided, "Okay. I want to make $100,000 in the next calendar year." Now at that time, Canfield was a schoolteacher, making $8,000 a year. The sum of $100,000 would be 12 times his income for the year—a seemingly impossible feat. But Canfield stayed in the question, *"What would you do if you just knew it wasn't impossible?"*

He made an over-sized $100,000 dollar bill, about three feet by two feet, which he put up on the ceiling above his bed. Every morning he'd wake up, see the bill, and say his affirmation, "God is my unlimited supply. May large sums of money come to me quickly and easily under the grace of God, for the highest good of all concerned. I am easily earning, saving and investing a $100,000 a year."

Whether he knew it or not, Canfield was behaving according to the fifth Commandment of Money:

You shall feel Higher Sensations.

If you look up the word Sensation, you'll find it means vibration, ambiance and atmosphere. When you feel Higher Sensations, you are creating an ambiance in and around you.

Your emotional involvement is what alters the vibration and sets up the attraction. Thought combined with feeling is a tremendous vibratory force. Jesus talks about this super power of the mind when he says [Proverbs 23:7], "As a man thinketh in his heart so is he." If you think with strong emotion about something long enough, whether it's something you want or don't want, it's going to come into your world.

Just saying an affirmation doesn't do any good. There must be feeling behind it. You have to support your affirmation with feelings, internalize it, in a sense become the actor and live the part. You must be emotionally involved with your affirmation, like Canfield.

Every day, Canfield would close his eyes, visualize and feel the sensation of living a $100,000 lifestyle. He would visualize and feel what his house would look like. What his car would look like. What charities he'd contribute to. And more. Then he would get up, take his shower and go about his day as a schoolteacher.

Now it so happened that Canfield had also written a little book called *A Hundred Ways to Enhance Self-Concept in the Classroom*, for which he received 25 cents every time it sold. After doing his visualization and emotionally charged affirmation process for a while, an idea popped into Jack's mind, "What if he could sell 400,000 copies of his book?" Four hundred thousand copies at a quarter each would add up to $100,000. He had no idea how he could bring such a thing about, nor did his publisher, but he was sure that if he simply stayed in the question, *"What would you do if you just knew it wasn't impossible?"* he would be shown a way.

Now, one thing I know for sure is that once you start visualizing and feeling the outcome, you'll start to see resources that were always there, that you never saw before, just as Canfield did. One day, he saw a Reader's Digest magazine that touted the number of its readers right on the cover. It had 37 million readers! Canfield thought for sure he could sell at least 400,000 copies of his book through them, but when he looked into putting an ad in Reader's Digest, it was beyond his budget.

Which brings us to the sixth Commandment of Money:

Thou shall get off thy But/Butt.

Both your "but" as in "impossible" and your "butt" as in "doing nothing." When you get guidance in the form of an idea, you must go into action. You cannot use "I would do that BUT" or "BUT that just won't work" as an excuse for not moving ahead with the idea.

Back to Canfield's story. A couple of weeks later, Canfield sees a National Enquirer at the supermarket, which had 12 million weekly readers. He promptly (no butt/buts!) called them up, but their ad rates were still more than he could afford. However, Canfield started incorporating both the Reader's Digest and National Enquirer into his daily practice of visualization and feeling.

Shortly thereafter, Canfield was asked to give a talk at a nearby college, where a woman approached him for an interview. When he asked her who she wrote for, she told him that as a freelancer, she wrote primarily for the National Enquirer. Canfield said he'd do the interview if she would include information on how people could get ahold of his book. She agreed. With that, his book sales took off! By the end of the year, after taxes, he made just a bit under $100,000. The rest of Canfield's career is well known. He's made over $1 million a year from his books and consulting practice.

How did all this happen for Canfield? Through what quantum physics calls "nonlocality." "Nonlocality describes the apparent ability of objects to instantaneously know about each other's state, even when separated by large distances almost as if the Universe at large instantaneously arranges its particles in anticipation of future events"—Physics of the Universe (physicsoftheuniverse.com/topics_quantum_nonlocality.html) Or what Albert Einstein called, "Spooky actions at a distance."

When you devote yourself to these Commandments, things begin to arrange and connect with ease and grace, which is precisely what happened to Canfield. He thought and felt that he was going to sell 400,000 books through the National Enquirer. He didn't know how, nor did he need to. You see, in nonlocality, the Universe makes the "how" happen.

In the absence of knowing anything about the "how," follow Canfield's example. Take a step in the direction of your goal/dream, no "but/butts" about it. Stay in your inquiring mind, and keep asking the question, "If I didn't think it was impossible, what would I do?" What you will find is that your higher vibrations will attract success almost effortlessly. Of course, you still have to *do* something, however you don't have to *force* anything.

Go with the flow of your intuition, and you will be led to new opportunities and people that in some way connect you to your success. Let the Universe, "nonlocality" do the rest.

12.

The 10 Commandments of Money - #7

Commandment #7:
You shall not spend time with or have people in your life that pull you down.

"There are certain laws which govern the process of acquiring riches, and once these laws are learned and obeyed, riches will come with mathematical certainty."
—Wallace Wattles

These laws are Universal. They have been used and taught by mystics and great teachers of the past and present, who all say, "These Laws work if you work them." You cannot apply the logic of the world to these laws. They are beyond our human understanding, indestructible and infinite. Most importantly, they work!

In this chapter, we will consider the two aspects of Universal law that underlie the seventh Commandment of Money. The first is that there lies within each of us an immense power. The second is that this power is impartial and indifferent.

The power within us is pure energy, a Life Force that is part of all things. You can call it God, Universal Mind, Christ consciousness or Buddha consciousness. What you call Life Force is irrelevant. What is important is that you identify with this power and learn to use it effectively.

This Life Force accepts whatever thoughts, feelings and declarations you project—and reflects them back to you. It gives you anything you believe in, no more and no less, without judgment or censure. Therefore, the key to understanding this aspect of Universal Law is to discover what your "money rejection complex" thoughts are, as we discussed in Chapter 9.

Some of these thoughts come from the collective unconscious, such as the belief that you can earn a certain amount of money and no more, or that you can only receive money by working at a nine-to-five job. Or that you are trapped by the circumstances under which you were born, with no way to break free. But the collective unconscious, as defined by Jungian psychology, is no more than the experience common to all mankind, which results in a group agreement to believe in unconscious decrees of sickness, poverty, lack, calamity and limitation, separate from and independent of one's own Higher Mind where all things are possible. And mastery, as Jesus taught us, is attained by being aware of the power of Spirit. Many people have refused to be a part of that collective unconscious, Oprah Winfrey being one of them, as illustrated by her stellar career, which by the dictates of the collective unconscious, should never have happened.

Understand that the collective unconscious agreements about money are all a matter of perception and belief. If you choose to believe and perceive what everyone else chooses to believe and perceive, you will get exactly that. Your attachment to the collective unconscious is what holds you back.

Our goal, as Unity students, is to rise above these attachments. In order to become part of a higher consciousness you must leave where you are right now in the collective unconscious and step into the unknown. As you move out of the world's group perception, you are going to see something pretty spectacular. You will see how systematically the Universe responds.

I love the example Stuart Wilde, author of *Life Was Never Meant To Be a Struggle*, gave during one of his classes, "You will see that the Universe works as a large mail order shipping company. The shipping company gets your order. If the order says 'size eight' the shipping company sends out a 'size eight.' It is of no concern to the shipping company whether 'size eight' fits you. The company merely complies with your request."

In your daily life, your feelings, thoughts and attitudes are your order form. Before you can change your present situation, you must be very sure what you want from life. You must be specific with your "order," because Universal Law reacts in a vague, unclear way to your vague, unclear "orders." Which is why a halfhearted commitment to a desired change will produce a halfhearted response.

Here's a small sample of the "orders" this Life Force gets on a daily basis:

You: "I really want to travel."

Life Force: "Great! I'd love to set that up for you, but it would be helpful to know where you want to go."

You: "Um, well, maybe the South of France. Or wait. No, I really want to go to the Caribbean. Except, no, I always wanted to salsa dance in Cuba. But wait, can I really afford it? Probably not."

Or you want a new car, but you fear that will mean higher payments. Or you want to be debt free, but don't believe that will ever happen. Or you want to commit to your new partner, but worry that he/she may leave you. These are the kind of messages the Universe gets all day, every day.

Every thought, feeling and vibration influences this Life Force and the only reason we don't have the manifestations we desire, is because our thoughts are scattered and lack focus. Instead of one, constant, well-aimed laser-like message to Life Force, our thoughts are like a bunch of kindergarteners playing soccer. Life Force is literally bouncing all over the place, trying to respond to our conflicting requests: "Go this way. No, wait, go that way." This amazing all-powerful Force that works with the certainty of mathematics is dissipated because we give it no clear direction on what we really want.

It's not that the Universe isn't fulfilling your intentions. It's that you're confusing it by intending too many completely opposite things. Give the Universe a break! It's your thoughts that need fine-tuning, not the Life Force.

One of the most notable stories about attracting money through using these principles is that of Cynthia Strafford, who won $112 million dollars in the lottery. In her many interviews, she shared her favorite book, *The Power of the Subconscious Mind* by Joseph Murphy. Strafford talks about how she didn't visualize, "Oh wouldn't it be nice to win the lottery." She visualized winning exactly $112 million dollars. Every time she would buy her lottery ticket, she didn't think, as so many people do, "Gosh, the odds of winning this are slim to none, but perhaps I could win, I could be the one. Wouldn't that be nice?" Strafford was *sure* she was going to win. She deliberately lived in wealth consciousness. Over and over again, she would say, "I am wealthy, I am wealthy," and she felt wealthy, despite the fact that neither her home nor her car reflected wealth. When Strafford won the lottery, it really wasn't a surprise to her because in her mind she had already won it.

Strafford would tell her many interviewers, "Wealth is an energy, just like poverty is an energy. Wealth will stay around you when you say you are wealthy. If you are uncomfortable with wealth, it won't stay, it will leave you! When you say you are poor, poverty will circulate in your life. What you put out will always come back."

Which bring us to our seventh Commandment of Money:

You shall not spend time with or have people in your life that pull you down.

In the memorable words of Peter Voogd, "If you hang around five confident people, you will be the sixth. If you hang around five intelligent people, you will be the sixth. If you hang around five millionaires, you will be the sixth. If you hang around five idiots, you will be the sixth. If you hang around five broke people, you will be the sixth. It's inevitable." I would add, if you hang around five dysfunctional people you will be the sixth!

The reason it's inevitable is that your vibration raises or drops according to the strongest energy frequency in your proximity. If the frequency of a group is higher than yours, then your vibrational frequency goes up. If it's lower, then your vibrational frequency goes down. Whatever strongest energy you are around is what you become. That is why going to Church is important. You are around people of like mind.

Surround yourself with people who pull you up. "Who you spend time with is who you become! Change your life by consciously choosing to surround yourself with people with higher standards!" says Tony Robbins. "You are the average of the five people you spend the most time with," says Jim Rohn.

If you tend to be surrounded by people who are poor, talk poor, who look at life from a "That's impossible" perspective, consider spending less time with them. I know this can be hard to do, from my own experience. When I was in my 20s and 30s, I clung to friendships with certain people far too long. All of them were great people, people I respected, but they had no concept of self-care or self-love. They were always in some kind of victimhood circumstance that they loved talking about. I would leave time spent in their presence feeling terrible. Gradually I was able to spend increasingly less time with them, and from that I learned that it is mandatory for my well-being to be among people who uplift me rather than among people who may drag me down. Just this simple step will shift your perspective of life.

There is a last component to the seventh Commandment of Money. Because most people subscribe to prevailing mass consciousness beliefs of lack and limitation, it is imperative that you "go and tell no man," as Jesus put it [Mark 7:36].

When you pursue a dream or goal, especially when it comes to money, inevitably you will run into people who doubt your abilities, question whether the dream is possible and even encourage you to settle for less. When you share a dream with people who infuse it with doubt, it causes you to second-guess yourself. It derails your laser beam intent and puts you back on the path of uncertainty and confusion. This in turn connects you with other hopeless minds. The result is that you feed each other and support each other with stories of setbacks and dissatisfactions.

Only share your dream with those who will believe in you and who will help to energetically feed your vision. Then none can pull you down vibrationally and the Life Force will be able to respond with precision to your clear and focused desire!

13.

⚬⚬⚬

The Ten Commandments of Money - #8

Commandment #8:

You shall not take your money out of circulation

Your fortune or lack of fortune is not the result of chance, but of the process of circulation. Good circulation impacts everything in our lives, from the condition of our bodies to the condition of our monetary affairs and more.

A healthy, vibrant body has good circulation—rich blood pumped by a strong heart at just the right pressure through unclogged blood vessels to your every cell and organ. When circulation is impaired, our bodies suffer in our brains, heart, liver, kidneys and limbs. The process of digestion requires the process of elimination, breathing in requires breathing out. All of life is about circulation. It is the truth with money as well.

As Paul states in Galatians 6:7, "Whatever a man sows, he will reap in return." Whatever you send out in circulation, whether in thought, word or action will return to you. What you give, you will receive. In *The Game of Life and How to Play It*, Florence Scovel Shinn writes, "If man gives hate, he will receive hate; if he gives love, he will receive love; if he gives criticism, he will receive criticism; if he lies, he will be lied to; if he cheats he will be cheated. What man gives, he will receive."

Two classic examples demonstrate this truth.

First, Howard Hughes. All he ever really wanted in life was more. He wanted more money, so he parlayed inherited wealth into a billion dollar pile of assets. He wanted more fame, so he broke into the Hollywood scene and soon became a film producer. He wanted the company of women, so he hired women to be with him. He wanted more thrills, so he designed, built and flew the fastest aircraft in the world. He wanted more power, so he secretly dealt political favors to two U.S. Presidents.

Yet this man concluded his life frightened, obsessed, paranoid and depressed. He became withered and dull, with a sunken chest, fingernails that had grown into grotesque corkscrews, rotting black teeth, tumors and needle marks from his drug addiction. Howard Hughes mistakenly worshipped "more." He needed more because in his mind there wasn't enough to satisfy him. He was dominated by a scarcity mentality, by the fear of "never enough." He sowed the seeds of "There isn't enough," and reaped their vibrational equivalency of misery and despair.

Another man, in another century, achieved an opulent life by sowing seeds of great enjoyment. His name was Lorenzo Ghiberti. He was an artist, born in Florence, Italy in 1378, where he died at the age of 87. Most of his artistic career was spent building six doors for the Baptistery in Florence. Six doors! That's it. The doors are bronze, in which are sculpted various Old and New Testament scenes with exquisite detail. Ghiberti's inspiration was the opulence that surrounded him in the form of the beautiful countryside, a good family and great support. The doors were his contribution, his gift, to God.

The first four doors took Ghiberti 21 years to complete. The last two doors— Michelangelo later called them the "Gates of Paradise"—took another 27 years to complete. His whole life was one of great joy because he continually planted seeds of appreciation and gratification. Ghiberti kept his time, talent and treasure in circulation without ever a thought to whether or not there was enough. He sowed seeds of goodness and reaped their vibrational equivalency of joy and abundance.

Today there's not much left of the Howard Hughes legacy except a huge wooden airplane that flew only once. But Ghiberti's "Gates of Paradise" still stand and are greatly admired, a magnificent testimony to his spiritual awareness of the opulence he lived in.

God said that on earth there will always be a "seedtime and harvest" [Genesis 8:22]. The seedtime is what you are giving, what you are sending into circulation. Giving activates receiving. The law at work behind the Eighth Commandment of Money is the law of giving and receiving. Giving makes you more productive. Even the young lad who gave his lunch of five loaves and two fish to Jesus, who then multiplied his gift to feed 5,000 hungry people, received in return "12 baskets full."

As Winston Churchill said, "We make a living by what we

get, but we make a life by what we give." The principle of giving and keeping things in good circulation has never failed me and nor will it fail you.

Giving serves the giver, many others, and returns to the giver multiplied! Make the giving principle real and personal in your life by testing it against every need you have—mental, physical, financial, social or spiritual. Give money joyfully and watch it come back multiplied. Give of your time and talent with love in your heart, and watch how your time, talents and love are bountifully returned.

The 10 Commandments of Money - #9 & #10

Commandment #9:
You shall be a good receiver.

Commandment #10:
You shall live each day in awe and gratitude.

These are the last two "10 Commandments of Money." These Commandments are meant to allow you to have ample amounts of money—an obvious necessity—so you can live on this physical plane without struggle or anxiety. With them, you raise your energy so that money can flow to you with ease. When you practice these principles, people and opportunities for more money will show up in your life in amazing ways.

The predominant thought about money in the collective unconscious is, "If I work really, really hard, I can make enough each week to have my essential needs met. Mortgage. Rent. Food on the table. Gas in the car." The only way out of the collective unconscious is for you to have a strength of will that is stronger than those dominant thoughts, and commit to these principles.

The Commandments may look simple, but they are not always easy to practice in the day to day of our lives. Have you ever been swimming in the ocean, when a big wave takes you down, and it takes all your might to swim to the top to catch your breath? It takes all your strength of will! It is the same with these 10 Commandments. The way of the world will say to you, "There isn't enough. There is only so much to go around. A limited amount of money or a limited amount of anything good, for a limited few."

What these Commandments offer is a way to swim to the top to catch your breath, and remember that God Force is absolutely abundant. There is no limit to God. There is no limit to God's abundance. There is only an ever-expanding amount of wealth. God will give you anything that you believe in and ask for, but you must be willing to commit to and practice these Commandments in order to rise above the collective unconscious and break through to God's Truth.

The truth is that you and I are here as Divine beings inside our earth suits. We have the ability, through our thought forms and through our feelings to absolutely redirect and change our lives.

The ninth Commandment of Money is:

You shall be a good receiver.

The problem is not to get God Force or the Universe to give you anything. God has nothing to give you. The Universe has nothing to give you. God has already given you *everything*. Right here, right now, you have everything you need. All that is required is for you to be a good receiver.

The practice of receiving is one of the most powerful tools you can use to attract more prosperity. As you rise above thoughts of lack and limitation, pay close attention to your ability to receive whatever good comes your way—gifts, hand-me-downs or anything else that is offered to you. Often we don't recognize prosperity in any other form than hard cash. Yet by refusing the good that is offered, no matter how large or small, we block the very flow of prosperity that we are asking for. We send an energetic message to the Universe about our unwillingness to receive!

Since everything is energy, when you pick up a penny from the sidewalk, when you say "yes" to someone's offer of a cup of coffee, you affirm that you are open to all the good that comes your way. Do not take this Commandment lightly, because it will help you to attract more money. As lottery winner Eddie Coronado, author of *Manifest Your Millions*, wrote, "The Universal law does not distinguish between a penny and million dollars, because it can easily give either." The Universe loves a good receiver!

Every day, practice accepting all the good that comes your way. Receive and let the energy and resources that flow into your life fill you with intense joy, contentment and gratitude. I personally learned a powerful lesson about receiving.

One day I wanted to buy a hair product from my hair

stylist. As I went to pay for the product, she refused, saying she wanted to gift it to me. I said, "Oh no. I want to pay you for this. I want to support your business." But she, being an enlightened soul, wouldn't allow that. She gave me a picture of a woman with open hands, with "One day, she decided to open her hands and receive" written on it. At that moment, I realized that I had not been a good receiver. I framed the picture and hung it in my office to remind me of this Commandment.

The tenth and final Commandment is:

You shall live each day in awe and gratitude.

A number of years ago a former Catholic priest, Ken Feit, came up with what he called his "Paper Bag Mass." The ceremony began in silence. Father Ken would set before him a brown paper bag filled with peculiar objects. The ritual consisted of taking these objects out of the bag one by one. As he reached into the bag, his face glowed with eager anticipation. When he pulled out, for example, a banana, his eyes opened wide in amazement. Father Ken looked at the banana in wonder, he sniffed it, pinched it, and his eyes lit up in delight and deep gratitude for the moment. Whereupon his congregation realized, it was no ordinary moment, but a special, wonderful, amazing one.

You see, the ordinary world is not very ordinary after all. Its seeming ordinariness is only a sign that our sensitivities have become dulled. Bananas no longer jump out at us and delight us with gratitude. The problem is not with the banana, it is with us. The banana is just as odd, amazing and mysterious as ever, but we have grown accustomed to bananas.

We have grown accustomed to the people we live with, accustomed to the car we drive, accustomed to the bed we sleep in. We have grown accustomed to our everyday lives. We don't stop to exclaim in wonder at all that fills our day. We are not amazed. We are not even moved to say, "Wow! It's great to be alive! I am so grateful right now!"

But when you are so very grateful to be alive and in awe of the moment, you can pull out of collective unconscious thoughts of lack and limitation within seconds. Being in gratitude unleashes tremendous spiritual powers of good.

As our Unity cofounder, Charles Fillmore, wrote in his book, *Jesus Christ Heals*, "A state of gratitude is the highest state that we can be in as a human being. When you express thanks, gratitude and praise, there is an energy released from the mind and SOUL which is usually followed by a profound effect and you become aware in the now moment that God is working in your life and that all is good. You can praise a weak body into strength, a fearful heart into peace and trust, shattered nerves into poise and power. It is a powerful insight to live by."

Charles Fillmore was right. Gratitude allows you to see the ordinary as extraordinary. Being grateful is central to the well-being of our daily lives. It should not be reserved only for what is new and shiny—your new car, new relationship, new baby, new job. Deliberately look at all the aspects of your life through the eyes of, "Wow! It is great to be alive! I am so grateful for what is right in front of me!"

Existence itself is full of wonder. It beckons each one of us forth to participate in life in an extraordinary way. Don't wait for things to be grateful for. Actively *search* for things to be grateful for, and express your feelings of gratitude in words. Make frequent positive and grateful comments to and about your friends, your spiritual community, your work, your family, your health, your home, your country, your life, and everything else you have been given. When all is going well in your life, express your gratitude. When all is not going so well in your life, deliberately express twice as much gratitude for anything you can find to be grateful for.

Work the Ten Commandments of Money and be amazed (and grateful!) at how powerfully they will work for you.

The 10 Commandments of Money:

#1: *You shall look to no other source but God as your supply!*

#2: *Thou shall not think that money is evil.*

#3: *You shall not speak the word of lack or limitation.*

#4: *You shall make no mental images of lack.*

#5: *You shall feel Higher Sensations.*

#6: *Thou shall get off thy But/Butt.*

#7: *You shall not spend time with or have people in your life that pull you down.*

#8: *You shall not take your money out of circulation.*

#9: *You shall be a good receiver.*

#10: *You shall live each day in awe and gratitude.*

15.

Thought + Feelings = Manifestation

H ave you ever wondered why some prayers are answered and others aren't? Why affirmations work for some people and not others? Why do we get what we get in life—or don't?

As I have watched people through the years, as well as in my own continual search for spiritual knowledge, I realize that there is one element we all have but don't always put it to good use. It is the fundamental element of the law of attraction. It is what Proverbs 23:7 means when it states, "As a man thinketh in his heart so is he."

If we think emotionally about something long enough, whether it's something we want or something we don't want, it is going to manifest in our world. Feeling follows thought, and we create by feeling. You see, a thought infused with feeling is energy, which in turn creates a vibrational frequency that the Universe responds to. For years, Unity has put it this way:

Thought + Feelings = Manifestation

Simple, yes. But not exactly easy.

I know two women, both of whom wanted to be debt free. Both of them owed a substantial amount of money in credit card debt. I observed how each of them went about their process. Both said their prayers and affirmations and both visualized the end result. After a period of time, one of the women was offered—completely out of the blue—a gift of sufficient money to pay off all her debt. The other woman is still trying to rid herself of debt but is starting to give up.

What made the difference? The woman who was able to pay off her debt set up an electromagnetic field of energy that attracted to her what she needed. She did this through her feelings. She infused her prayers, her affirmations and her visualizations with feelings of being debt free—with feelings that somehow God was coming through for her. In so doing, she was vibrating at a higher frequency.

The other woman was vibrating at a lower frequency. She entertained thoughts of lack, which sabotaged her earnest prayers and affirmations. For example, whenever she would hear about others paying off their debt, she would think, "I don't know if that will ever happen to me," or "How I envy people who can do that!" Such thoughts and feelings of lack keep us from our dreams and desires.

For example, people who want a significant other in their lives sometimes do all the work of writing down what they want in a partner. They pray and affirm, they even go to places where they could meet someone or engage in online dating. But as soon as such people see a happy couple they are envious, resentful and upset that they don't have that in their lives. Such people are vibrating at a lower frequency, because they have veered away from their intent. They've allowed negative feelings to get in the way of their stated desire.

The Universe is always saying, "Yes," but what is it saying yes to? The feeling, what you "thinketh in your heart." The feeling is what will bring your desire into manifestation. Your feelings are energetic. They are what create your vibration. It has been said for many years that it only takes 16 seconds to link up vibrationally to whatever we're focused on. Only 16 seconds of pure, focused thought and feeling, whether it is good or bad, positive or negative.

In that brief time, we start to vibrate at the same frequency as whatever it is we've been emotionally thinking about, which means we will attract that thing if we keep it up. Now it may not be that we attract the exact thing that we are thinking and feeling about, but since like attracts like, we will certainly attract something of like vibration. It's similar to what happens with a tuning fork. You ding one and all the others of matching frequency vibrate right along with it, without your touching them.

The same thing happens with our thoughts. As you think and feel more and more about something, you're not only attracting whatever it is that you're thinking about, you're pulling in anything else that just happens to be of a similar frequency. For example, some years ago I got three speeding tickets in one day! Before that, I had never received a ticket in my entire driving career of some 20 years! At the time, I was going through a divorce, and on that particular day I woke up with angry thoughts. I was definitely vibrating at a low frequency. As I drove out of town to go to an appointment in the next town over, I got a ticket—which made me vibrate at even a lower frequency. Once I got to the next town, I got another ticket, which made me vibrate at even a lower frequency, only to get one more ticket on my way home that night. Three tickets in one low-frequency day that I allowed to go from low frequency to lower to lowest.

This is why it is so important that we pay attention to where we focus our energy! Because if we continue to focus on what is wrong with everybody and everything, those low vibrational thoughts will never bring us the life we desire. It will only bring more of whatever it is that we want so desperately to change. But how do we change this? We certainly can't watch everything that we think all day long.

Don't worry. It's easier than you think. Your feelings will tell you if something is off course. All you have to do is pay attention to how a thought or situation makes you feel. As long as we are on this planet, we are going to experience "down days," when nothing is going right. Know that it is not a big deal. Give yourself permission to experience the whole gosh darn downer of a day. You don't have to stuff your feelings, let them have a voice.

However, when you are ready to get out of the downer, there are steps you can take to bring up your vibratory frequency. For it isn't the occasional negative thought or dark feeling that will cause you to vibrate at a lower frequency, it's keeping those thoughts or feelings going and going and going.

The first step you can take when you become aware of an unwanted thought or feeling is to say to yourself, "Cancel clear." This first step is very basic to New Thought, yet we don't always do it. If something slips out like, "I can't afford that," say to yourself, "Cancel clear that thought." What you are telling the Universe when you do this, is that this is not what you want to have manifest in your life. Sometimes I yell, "Cancel clear" out loud, and if I forgot to roll up the car window, those who are not familiar with the concept must think I'm a lunatic!

The second step is to change your vibrational frequency. Sometimes taking a walk or doing something physical can change your focus from what you don't want to what you do want. Or deliberately thinking of persons or situations that make you feel good, like thinking of someone you love and adore. As you find ways to feel a tiny bit better than before, one little feeling at a time, you begin reversing what could otherwise become a lifetime of negative attraction.

The third step is to intend. An intention is not only a desire, it is the use of your will. Intention opens up new and much needed energy pathways. As Gary Zukaf states in *The Seat of The Soul*, "You create your reality with your intentions. How does this happen? Intentions set energy into motion, it sets patterns into motion." Every experience and every change in your experience reflects an intention.

Think of intending as a combination of "I want and I expect." For example, notice the difference in how you feel when you say, "I want a relationship" versus "I intend to have a new relationship." Or "I want a new car" versus "I intend to have a new car." Or "I want a full bank account," versus "I intend to have a full bank account." You can feel the strength in your intention. You can feel the authority, the force of command and the power behind every intention.

Intending helps direct our energy to a higher frequency, which draws to us higher frequency experiences and opportunities. Intending on a daily basis is a most valuable practice! Here are some intentions to get you started. Add other intentions specific to your life and desires.

I intend to feel joy this day.

I intend to feel in love with my life.

I intend to find happiness in all that I do.

I intend to have a deeper spiritual connection with God.

16.

First, Second and Third Force

A number of years ago I came across a teaching from two Russian philosophers, Pyotr Demianovich Ouspenskii and George Gurdjieff, who in the 1920s wrote a series of books collectively called *The Work*. Among the many valuable teachings in *The Work* is called "The Law of Three."

Ouspenskii and Gurdjieff believed that the Universe operates under the "Law of Three." For example, there is the Father, Son and the Holy Ghost; mind, idea and manifestation; a baby develops over a period of three trimesters; a year is made up of 12 months— which is four times three. Given this law, Ouspenskii and Gurdjieff believed that there are three forces at work in the Universe: First, Second and Third Force.

First Force is wanting something. For example, let's say your desire is to buy a new house. First Force is an active energy. You are active as you put your desire out to the Universe. You say your affirmations, you pray—and all of the sudden you meet up with Second Force.

Second Force are those things that oppose your desire. You put out that you want a new house but you find out that your credit isn't as good as you need it to be. Or there are more things wrong with the house than you anticipated. Second Force are those things that seem to be in the way of what you want. However, once you get through Second Force, you come into Third Force, which is the manifestation of your original idea but even better than you could imagine.

Back to our house example. Maybe the house you originally wanted fell through, so back you go house-hunting. Guess what? You find the house of your dreams. All of a sudden, doors begin to open that were apparently shut (your credit is sufficient!), and you are able to purchase this new house with ease and grace.

The problem is that many people stay stuck in Second Force, a place of resistance. They live their lives there and wonder why their desires are never fulfilled. Therefore, it's very important, if you want to live the life you dream of, to get through Second Force. But how?

You become nonresistant.

Jesus continually made statements referring to this very thing when he said:

"Agree with thine adversary quickly."

"Love your enemies and do good unto them that hurt you."

"If a man strikes you on one side of the cheek, turn also the other."

"Resist not evil."

"Pray for those who spitefully use you."

These are pretty tall orders for us to practice on an everyday basis. Non-resistance is hard! It's hard when you're in conflict with someone and want to be right. It's hard when you are going through trials and tribulations. And it is certainly hard when there is something you want so much and it is just not coming about.

So when Jesus says "Resist not evil," or "Agree with thine adversary quickly," what the heck is he saying? He is indicating the need to elevate our thoughts about the person or the situation. Because as we know, we cannot solve our problem from the same level of consciousness in which the problem exists. We must rise to a higher state of consciousness than that of the problem. And when we do this, the answers, solutions and resolutions will be revealed to us. It is in the very midst of our problems that it is essential to rise to a higher state of consciousness.

One time, when the Winter Olympics were in Salt Lake City, a friend and I wanted to go see the medals ceremony. The only thing was, we didn't have tickets and they were hard to come by. So we stood outside the event (I felt like I was at a Grateful Dead concert) asking people if they had tickets that we could buy. We got sneered at and laughed at, until finally we let go (non-resistance) and let God take over. We decided that if we were going to get in, we would, and if not, then we would do something else. No matter what happened, we would be Divinely guided.

Suddenly, out of seemingly nowhere, a couple came up to us and asked us if we wanted to buy their tickets—at half the face value! Thrilled, we bought the tickets, having no idea where the seats were. Imagine our surprise when we discovered our seats were right in front of the stage! We were as up close and personal as we could get. Not only that, I caught the bouquet of two-dozen yellow roses one of the gold medalists tossed out to the crowd. Incredible things happen when you choose not stay in Second Force. We are constantly given opportunities to go to a higher level of consciousness, let go of our will and let something bigger take over.

The true test is whether you can hold yourself steadily non-resistant toward an apparent injustice directed at you. If you do not resist, the act is not unjust to you, because you do not receive it that way. The act belongs to the other person, and you let the Universe handle Divine justice. Which it always does. As you value your peace of mind, your well-being, you will take steps that are guided by a Higher Power, rather than by your personal will.

But "resist not" seems like a paradox, doesn't it? It appears to be contrary to everything that is natural to us. When something is done to us, when something or someone opposes us, we meet that person, that circumstance, that condition, with every force we have. We do everything we know how to do to break down that opposition. That is why most people stay in Second Force. It becomes how they live.

I'm here to tell you that resistance brings you no gain. If you resist by active opposition, which means through your anger, through wanting to hurt someone, through your resentment, fear, frustration, through your impatience, you hold on to what you resist.

In Unity we say, "What you resist, persists." To resist means to fight, to struggle or to oppose. It seems that only when we are up against a wall are we willing to let go of our resistance. Only then do we let the Holy Spirit have its way with us. Only then do we see that there is a bigger design.

A life of nonresistance is not for sissies. Non-resistance is for those who are strong and who are dedicated to a life filled with purpose. Most certainly, non-resistance does not mean that you become a doormat. It means that you rise to a higher level of consciousness where you are present with God. That presence of God will then move you through the situation (through Second Force) and you will be able to follow your God-given intuition to do what is appropriate.

A friend of mine, Alice, had a really strained relationship with her mother. Alice's dream was to have a loving relationship with her mother (First Force). For years something always came up that would cause the two of them to disagree and argue (Second Force). Their resistance showed up as always having to be right, and making the other person wrong. They both ended up hurt and disappointed.

Alice then came across this teaching and realized that she had been living in Second Force. She remembered Jesus' teaching, "Agree with thine adversary quickly." Alice decided that she didn't have be right all the time. She decided that she was just going to agree with whatever her mother had to say. Her next phone call to her mother went something like this:

Mother: "You're spending too much money on this call."

Alice: "Yeah, you're probably right, Mom."

Mother: "That man you married is totally wrong for you."

Alice: "Yeah, you're probably right, Mom."

Mom: "Colorado is no good for you, you should be back here in Ohio."

Alice: "Yeah, you're probably right, Mom."

Agreeing with her mother didn't mean that Alice was going to do whatever her mother said. She was still going to do her own thing. She was just allowing her mother to be right. Alice told me that her mother finally broke down, started crying and said, "I am so sorry with how I have treated you. I love you so much, and I guess I just don't know how to show it." It was the first time Alice had ever heard the words "I love you" from her mother. They had moved past Second Force into a miracle of Third Force, "I love you."

You see, all pain is born out of resistance. Wherever there is pain, whether it is physical, emotional, mental, or spiritual, you can be sure that there is resistance behind it. The way to free yourself of pain is to let go of resistance.

Often we resist simply by worrying. I've certainly been known to do my fair share of worrying. I'm sure that if worrying were a paying job, we'd all be rich by now! But worrying can take up so much space in our minds that there isn't room to be happy. Somehow we get stuck on the idea that if we were to stop worrying, something dreadful would happen. We worry almost as if worry were an insurance policy.

- If we worry enough about being poor—we won't be.
- If we worry enough about our loved ones' safety—no harm will come to them.
- If we worry enough about our job—we won't get fired.

Aren't your worries always about what might or what might not happen? You worry about how to send your kids to college. You worry about test results. You worry about how to pay off your credit cards. In every case you project yourself into the future and imagine something bad happening. You start resisting something before it may or may not become a fact. You create a Second Force and proceed to live there.

Resistance comes from our personal will, from our need to control and manipulate. If we let our personal will and our negative emotions be in control, we will always be led astray. Resistance is hell, for it places us in a state of torment. Isn't it better to feel free and happy than to be attached to pain? Move with the flow! Surrender to an energy and a power that is greater than yourself. Ride the river of life, instead of fighting it and getting pulled under.

If you want to live a life that is incredibly rewarding, practice letting go of resistance. Go to a higher level of consciousness than that of the particular thing that you are resisting, and let God guide you through Second Force to the fulfillment and joy of Third Force!

17.

Only Three Feet From Gold?!

Napoleon Hill interviewed a millionaire by the name of R.U. Darby when Hill was doing the research for what was to become his most famous book, *Think and Grow Rich*. Darby told Hill about his uncle, who back in the 1850s, was caught by the gold-rush fever. The uncle went west to "dig and grow rich" in the mining business.

Now, Darby's uncle didn't know anything about mining. He'd never studied mining. He just wanted to find gold. So, he staked a claim and went to work with his pick and shovel. After weeks of hard manual labor, he struck gold—lots of it! Just one little problem—the uncle wasn't prepared for his newfound fortune. He needed machinery to remove the enormous amount of rocks and dirt. However, such machinery cost money that the uncle didn't have, so he carefully covered up his mine and went home to Williamsburg, Maryland.

Darby's uncle announced his great discovery and bragged to all of the tremendous wealth of gold that lay in the ground just waiting for his return. It didn't take long to persuade his family and friends to invest in the needed equipment. Money in hand, the uncle, joined now by his nephew, Darby, returned to California for the promised treasure.

The first gold rocks retrieved were analyzed, and sure enough, they contained high-quality ore. Just a few more loads, and Darby and his uncle would not only be able to repay their debts to their family and friends, but would have plenty of money to spare. Then tragedy struck. The gold disappeared. They kept digging and digging and digging, but no more gold was found. Finally, their dissatisfaction and impatience got the best of them and they decided to quit.

Discouraged and defeated, Darby and his uncle sold both the mine and their equipment to a local junkman for just a few hundred dollars. With that, Darby and his uncle took the next train home in Maryland, ending their quest for gold.

For years, this junkman had been looking for an opportunity to break into the mining industry. It was his dream. You see, the junkman was passionate about the idea of mining. It was something that he visualized and thought about all the time. He had studied mining for over a decade and always believed it was his destiny. He was just waiting for the right opportunity.

But the story doesn't end there. The junkman was smarter than most people gave him credit for. Deed in hand, he hired a mining engineer to inspect the claim. Together they discovered what is known as a fault line. The engineer explained that gold ran in long veins and that the previous owners had only drilled through one side of the vein. He explained that if the junkman were to go back and dig in the other direction, vertically to where the Darbys had made their first discovery, he would most likely tap back into the treasure.

The junkman followed these simple instructions and, sure enough, he hit one of the largest pockets of ore ever uncovered—a mere three feet away from where the Darbys had quit mining. He retrieved millions of dollars in gold from the site. The junkman succeeded where Darby and his uncle had failed because of two things—his determination to fulfill his dream and vision of becoming a gold miner and, of course, his willingness to seek expert advice.

There is even more to this story, but let's examine this story so far and how it may apply to each of us.

There are times when people come to me for spiritual counseling and they say something like, "I've done everything on the spiritual level. I say my affirmations, visualize, pray and meditate and nothing happens. In fact, my life has gotten worse!" Even though I reassure them that their prayers and requests are going out like heavenly rockets, and the Universe is on the verge of delivering great manifestations, they get impatient and discouraged and go back to old thoughts forms, old patterns and old ways of living. They give up on their dreams and ambitions.

They doubt the Universal Truths—Truths that have no other choice but to work. Sometimes they leave Unity and its principles all together, never to return. Ask any New Thought Minister and they will tell you the same tale.

People like the Darbys quit because they are not committed to their vision. As Napoleon Hill wrote, "Before great success comes, you will surely meet with temporary defeat. When people are overtaken by these feelings, the easiest and perhaps most logical thing to do is to quit. Quitting is exactly what the majority of people do." The junkman had a vision that he was committed to. The junkman who turned into a multimillionaire always knew, in his heart of hearts, that one day he would catch his break and become a gold miner, and so he did whatever he needed to do until that opportunity arose. Because the Universe has no other choice but to deliver, one day, he was in the right place at the right time to come upon someone who practically gave him everything he needed to achieve his dream.

The junkman had "stickability." He was not just interested in his vision, he was committed to his vision, which made all the difference. The junkman had the ability to stick with his dream despite what Hill calls "temporary defeat."

For example, have you ever tried to achieve something in your life—you have an intention, a vision, a goal that you feel great about—but then you are met with resistance? Or perhaps you experienced some kind of upheaval and simply didn't want to go on. When you are met with resistance or an upheaval, opposition of any kind, quite possibly you are experiencing what Unity calls "chemicalization."

Chemicalization is what happens when there is a re-ordering of your life to accommodate the manifestation you seek. It's the shifting around, making room for and cleaning up of your thoughts and beliefs that prepare you for the change about to occur. Chemicalization is the process of transformation. It is a Spiritual Sodium Bi-Carb moment.

Sodium Bi-Carbs are a great metaphor for the "percolating

up" of old belief systems and self-defeating assumptions that we allow to limit our good. As we grow on our spiritual journeys, we are bound to run into moments when our old beliefs run head-on into our new-ways of thinking. When you go through a chemicalization experience, it is sign of growth, not stagnation or backsliding. It is not the time to give up or throw in the towel! It is not the time to be impatient, but rather to recommit to your vision. The old thoughts and beliefs that have kept you unaware of who you really are and what you can really do are undergoing a revolutionary change. You are rising to a higher octave in consciousness, to a higher vibratory frequency.

One of the most common causes of failure is quitting when one is overtaken by temporary defeat, not realizing that you might just be going through a re-shifting in consciousness to make room for your desired manifestation. Whenever you feel like giving up on your dream, remember that you may be just three feet from gold!

Even Norman Vincent Peale knew temporary defeat. His dream was to publish his manuscript, *The Power of Positive Thinking*, but he grew discouraged after it was rejected by publisher after publisher. He began to listen to the old voices in his head. All his limiting beliefs came up to the surface. He didn't understand that they only bubbled up in order to be cleaned out. He gave up, threw his manuscript in the wastebasket, but his wife refused to let him stop there. She fished out the manuscript and urged him to send it out one more time. Sure enough, that last publisher accepted his manuscript, which went on to sell more than 25 million copies in 42 languages. To this day, it remains a best seller.

Every time you aim higher, it involves a tussle with your

limiting beliefs of the past. Too many times, we give up when we listen to the old voices in our heads. Those voices can say things like, "Who are you to think you could succeed at this? What makes you think you can do it when you've never made it happen before? What makes you think you could be healthy/ abundant when you've known so much poor health/lack of abundance? A miracle? Get over it. That doesn't happen in real life. Even if it did, it wouldn't last. You simply don't deserve it."

Yet often, just one more step is all it takes, but we don't see this because we are too preoccupied with the challenge itself, not trusting that the Universe is always working on our behalf. Just because you don't know how it's going to happen, doesn't mean it isn't going to happen. Our job is to commit to our dream; the Universe's job is to arrange circumstances and events for our dreams to come true.

As you go through the mystical process of chemicalization, with its seeming upsets and upheavals, say to yourself, "I believe. I am open to receive. I am committing to this vision or something better and I will not quit, for I may just be—three feet from gold."

18.

Choose Your Focus

U nity is for the willing, the goodhearted and the sane. You may wonder about the "sane" part, but that will be explained later.

Charles Fillmore, co-founder of Unity, stated that in Unity, there is only one code of belief, one doctrine, and that is to look for the good. To look for the good in all situations, to look for the good in each other and to look for the good in ourselves.

When you are feeling doubtful, fearful or concerned about something, do you look for the good? When you are discouraged or dismayed, do you look for the good? It is a simple practice but not always easy to accomplish.

When I was at Unity Village in Missouri for meetings, I ran into an old friend, Rev. Festus Umeojiego, who reminded me of this doctrine. As a Nigerian refugee many years ago, Festus had suddenly found himself without a home, family or any means of supporting himself. As he searched for what to do, he crossed paths with a man who gave him a copy of the *Daily Word*, and said, "These people are your new family. They are praying for you night and day." Festus took those words to heart and managed to travel to the United States and attend a Unity Church. Later, he attended Ministerial school from which he and I graduated together. Festus has made a profound difference in countless lives.

Not all looks good, but good comes from all.

Another friend, Edwene Gaines, was a newlywed when her husband was transferred to China. Once there, Edwene found out that she was pregnant. She was thrilled. Her husband, less so. As soon as Edwene shared the happy news, he left her. She was in a foreign country with no means to get back to the States, penniless and unable to speak the language. Someone gave her a Unity *Prosperity* book. She promptly put the principles in the book to work. Edwene is now one of the most prosperous women I know, a successful author (*The Four Spiritual Laws of Prosperity*) who travels around the world teaching prosperity workshops.

Not all looks good, but good comes from all.

There are always two ways of looking at every situation. One view brings confidence, success and joy, the other brings doubt, failure and discontent. When you look at a situation you may see it as drudgery, or you may see it as an opportunity leading to something good. The spiritual path asks you to look for the good in *all* situations. That means no matter how difficult, insurmountable or overwhelming a situation or circumstance appears, whether you can see how this is possible, good is in it.

Jesus said, "Judge not by appearances." It makes no difference what the appearance might be, you are being asked to go beyond the appearance in the face of all that is before you, whether it be outer conflict or inner confusion. When you go beyond appearances, you hold true to the vision of going forward toward the good. You begin to see what is truly important.

That awkward situation that happened yesterday and the bruised feelings you experienced, was it really important after all? That failure you suffered or that mistake you made last year, is it important today? Could any experience be significant enough to rob you of going forward and claiming your good for today?

Now that does not mean that if you are in an abusive situation, you stay in it and look for the good. If you are in an abusive situation, that is not taking care of yourself. Your self-worth must govern your decisions. In this case, look for the good in your next steps out of that abusive situation.

If you think of yourself as a victim of negative experiences in your life, you have forgotten that in God all things work together for good. A rainy, foggy, day may be either a disappointment or an opportunity to read and enjoy yourself. A relationship that is fraught with challenges may be either a bummer, or an opportunity to work through the challenges into something beautiful. We can see the good just as easily as we can see adversity.

It's all about where we choose to focus. Look for the good and act according to God's divine plan. The Universe is poised to give you great good! Time after time, I have seen people lose their jobs, or their spouses or their world seemed to be crumbling around them, yet once they have adopted this one principle and looked for the good, miracles happened.

At times when there are difficulties in our lives, it may

seem easy to become discouraged, to become lax in using this principle. Certainly, we all have our times of ranting and raving, including me, but neither you nor I can afford the luxury of staying in our negativity.

If your life is going along splendidly now, wonderful! File this principle in your mind for future reference, because there will undoubtedly come a time when an unfortunate experience will occur, and you will need to remember that God's good is present in all circumstances. Then you will need to step away from the lack, step away from your doubt, your fear, your concern, your worry, and hold your vision higher.

Now, contrary to popular belief, your good does not come from you or your hard work. It does not come from your boss, or your clients, or your spouse, or the public. It does not come from luck, or gambling, or even Aunt Martha's will (just in case you are waiting to collect an inheritance). Your good comes from one source, and one source only, God. Do you think you can work hard enough to achieve in a lifetime what the Universe can give you in an instant? It is not possible. God is the life giver, the sustainer and the provider. For thousands of years we have been told "Ask and you will receive." You see, there is no shortage of supply, there is only a shortage of demand. We normally don't ask for our good!

Unbelievably, most people do not expect to receive good. One of the most difficult things for many is simply to accept their good. Many of us have been conditioned to believe that the other shoe is going to fall at anytime and that we are not worthy of getting what you really want. That we are destined to struggle in this life. But here's the thing. If you refuse the good that you are offered, you are refusing God. Not a good idea to pray for something and refuse it at the same time! As with Rev. Festus Umeojiego and Edwene Gaines, you never know where your good is coming from. It can come from channels both known and unknown, for God truly works in mysterious ways. Be open to His ways!

Your good precedes you. It's already there before you get there. Your job is to move in the direction of your good, the good that God makes available to you at all times. However, in order to catch up with your good, you must have ears that hear and eyes to see or it will escape you. Some people never catch up with their good. They say, "My life has always been one big hardship, how can good ever come out of this?" You must be awake to the opportunities that God puts along your path and claim your good.

Unity is for the willing, the goodhearted and the sane, because the average person will dwell on the obstacles until the situation grows worse and worse. That kind of thinking *will* drive you insane. Don't give in to the insanity! Look away from adverse appearances and give God your undivided attention.

Know, without a doubt, that the entire Universe is lined up just to make sure your life is good, and to ensure your well-being.

Casual Attire Sunday

I was packing some of my belongings because I had taken an interim position at a Church out of state. I suddenly realized I had packed all my nicer, dressier clothes and had left nothing for my last Sunday service at my home Church. Oy vey! What was I thinking? I should have planned ahead!

With that, I promptly went into struggle mode. I could go back into the boxes and find something for the coming Sunday, which meant opening box after box, probably having to iron something and who knows what else. In the midst of my turmoil, the thought hit me; I could struggle less and look at another possibility. What about if we just had a "Casual Attire Sunday"?

My struggle reminded me vividly how much of our lives we spend looking through the problem/struggle lens instead of looking at life through the possibility lens. As long as we keep focusing on all the things that we think are not right, we will continue to attract that which is not right. So turn it off! Stop looking through the problem/struggle lens.

The next time you feel a sense of strain, or find yourself struggling, ask yourself if it really has to be this hard, or if you are *making* it hard. Back off, take a higher view and then keep your focus firmly on allowing the Universe to bring you something bigger and better.

Remember that nothing is happening *to* you. It's all happening *for* you. Be flexible, go with the flow and allow the Universe to give you an idea that is beyond your current thought process.

Welcome to Casual Attire Sunday!

19.

Let Go of Your "Story"

Mason Wells was cheering his mom at the Boston Marathon in 2013 when the bomb exploded that took the lives of three spectators and wounded 260 others. Although he wasn't injured, a mere three years later, in 2016, Wells was one of those severely wounded in the bomb attack on the Brussels' International Airport that killed 32 people and wounded 300.

Once recovered, Wells released a video message to the attackers, stating that although their acts were evil and that he retains the scars to this day, he chose to forgive them. By his decision to forgive and get past the events of that day, Wells says that he became a stronger person. He had chose to live not in fear, but to be grateful for each day. This, from the survivor of not one, but two horrific bombings.

Had Mason Wells developed a taste for revenge and hatred,

those emotions surely would have damaged his soul. He would have allowed an evil act to have a permanent victory. We take a tremendous step toward freedom and awakening when we forgive those people or circumstances that have brought us pain. Forgiveness is a difficult practice. It requires strength and fearlessness and courage. For to let go of the ones who might have hurt us is also to let go of a part of our identity.

You see, our identity is often caught up in the role of the victim. We tend to justify our victimhood through the "story" we tell ourselves and anyone else who will listen. However, in the process we undermine ourselves and stay stuck in the past. When we live our lives based on this "story," we are essentially living an illusion because the truth of who you are is not a victim. You are much bigger than that.

It is only as we forgive and let go of our "story," that we are set free from the endless cycle of pain, anger, blame and judgment that keeps us imprisoned. Sometimes we need to forgive others, those who hurt us. Sometimes we need to forgive ourselves. Forgiveness is required of us in rich measure, even when our wounds are painful. It is forgiveness that heals the pain, that allows us to grow in heart and spirit.

When we sing the Lord's Prayer on Sundays we ask "to forgive us our trespasses, as we forgive those who trespass against us." We are then born fresh into this moment, unencumbered by the struggles of our old stories. It can feel like the bad guys are getting off scot-free, while we are left with all the pain. But forgiveness is not primarily for them, forgiveness is first and foremost for us.

Jack Kornfield, the great Buddhist teacher, went with Maha

Gosananda, a respected Cambodian monk, into the refugee camps where thousands of Cambodians had fled the terrible holocaust conducted by Pol Pot. Maha Gosananda announced to the refugees that there would be a Buddhist ceremony the next day and all who wished to come were welcome. The tens of thousands of refugees who congregated the next day were eager and curious to hear what Maha Gosananda would say.

Having opened the ceremony with traditional Buddhist invocations, Maha Gosananda chanted a verse from the Buddhist scripture:

Hatred never ceases by hatred;

But by love alone is healed.

This is an ancient and eternal law.

Over and over again Maha Gosananda chanted this verse, among the tens of thousands people gathered who had great cause to hate. Yet as he sat there, repeatedly chanting this verse, one by one, thousands of voices joined together and chanted the verse in unison.

Out of the mouths of people who had been made homeless, who had been wounded physically and emotionally, demoralized and crushed by the pain of war, came a prayer that was much bigger than their victimhood, a prayer that was much greater than all the sorrows they had seen and felt. It took tremendous courage for them to go to that place of forgiveness. For as the Bhagavad-Gita states, "If you want to see the brave, look at those who can forgive, of you want to see the heroic, look at those who can love in return for hatred." As long as we harbor thoughts of revenge or anger in our hearts, hatred will never cease in this world, for peace on this planet begins with each of us individually.

Forgiveness can be hard, and for some the journey toward forgiveness can be long and difficult. I remember a time when I was really mad at someone. I was told to forgive, but I just couldn't. My Ministerial teacher told me, "Then don't forgive. You are not ready to forgive yet. You must go through the anger and let that anger out, but be *willing* to forgive when you are ready. The heart knows when it is ready to forgive. "

Many stay in the anger instead of moving *through* the anger. The first step is to allow the expression of our anger in a safe and appropriate way, often through physical exercise or by writing it out. After that, all you need is the *willingness* to forgive, because then the actual process of how to forgive becomes doable. Provided that you desire to forgive your offender, the greater part of the work is already done.

Many people think that forgiveness means that you excuse or condone bad behavior. Not so! Forgiveness is simply a way to lay down the burden of judgment and hurt that you are carrying so you can move on.

Here is a process for forgiveness:

1. Make sure that you are ready to forgive. You may need time to get out your anger and resentment. Forgiveness has its own timing; it should be nurtured and invited, but never forced.

2. Get by yourself and become quiet.

3. Have a moment of prayer with God.

4. Then quietly say;

   "I fully and freely forgive _____; I loose him/
   her and let him/her go. I completely forgive the whole
   incident in question. As far as I am concerned, it is
   finished forever. I cast the burden of resentment upon
   the Christ Light. He/she is now free, and I am free
   too. The Christ Light has set us both free and that
   incident is now finished. I thank God."

5. Then get up and go about your business. Let the forgiveness process do its work.

If the person who offended you comes up again in your
mind, bless him or her and dismiss the thought. Do this however many times the thought may come back to you. After a
few days, the thought will return less and less often, until you
forget it altogether.

A daily practice of forgiveness can also be very beneficial.
For example, when you say your daily prayers, issue a general
reprieve: "If anyone has harmed me knowingly or unknowingly
in thought, word or deed, I freely forgive them. And if I have
harmed anyone knowingly or unknowingly in thought, word
or deed, I freely forgive myself."

As a result of this practice you will find yourself quickly
cleared of all resentment and condemnation, and the effect upon
your happiness, your health and your general life will be nothing
less than glorious.

20.

⬤⬤⬤

Blessed Are Those Who Go Through Chaos for They Shall See Order

Have you ever experienced times when you thought you were going insane? I have. Which is why I could relate to an e-mail I received relaying an out-going message for a Mental Health Hotline. This is what it said:

"Hello and welcome to the Mental Health Hotline.

If you obsessive-compulsive, press one repeatedly.

If you are co-dependent, ask someone to press 2 for you.

If you have multiple personalities, press 3, 4, 5, 6.

If you are paranoid, we know who you are and what you want. Just stay on the line and we'll trace your call.

If you are delusional, press 7 and your call will be transferred to the Mother Ship.

If you are schizophrenic, listen carefully to that small voice and it will tell you which number to press.

If you are depressed, it doesn't matter which key you press—no one will answer your call.

If you are dyslexic, press 69696969.

If you have a nervous disorder, please fidget with the pound key and wait for the beep—after the beep—please wait for the beep.

If you have short term memory loss, please try your call again later.

And if you have low self-esteem, hang up. Our system is overloaded and no on can talk to you right now."

Now be honest, haven't there been times when you have been co-dependent, depressed, delusional, paranoid or suffered low self-esteem? I certainly have! A teacher of mine used to say, "Insanity comes right before transformation." I would have to agree. Chaos is a precursor to change.

A bird who sheltered each day in the withered braches of a tree that stood in the middle of a vast deserted plain. There, he seemed happy for he knew no other way. One day, a whirlwind uprooted the tree, forcing the poor bird to fly one hundred miles in search of shelter. Eventually, the bird came to a forest of trees full of fruit and other wonderful pleasures. If the withered tree had survived, nothing would have induced the bird to give up its security and fly to this paradise!

How many times have we been uprooted by a whirlwind

or in a state of chaos, when it seems as though those things which at one time brought us security are no longer around, or serving us? Well, that's the way life can be—and in a way, that's the way life *should* be, for chaos is a fundamental impulse of the Universe.

Although we as humans tend to detest chaos and avoid it whenever possible, nature uses chaos in remarkable ways to create new events and shape new life that holds the Universe together. Not long ago, the Hubble Space Telescope took a photo of the collision between two galaxies. Just like a pebble thrown into a lake, this violent encounter flung a violent ripple of energy into space, plowing gas and powder before it at 200,000 miles per hour. To most of us, this would sound like the traditional idea of chaos, yet within the hot ring of gasses, billions of new stars were being born—a perfect illustration that chaos is both the death of the old and the birth of a new.

Science recognizes chaos theory, which tells us that creation emerges out of the unpredictable events of our lives—that beneath the frenzy of disorder lies a pattern, an interconnectedness, from which all order evolves. Chaos theory suggests that instead of resisting life's uncertainties, we should embrace them.

Chaos can give us life-changing lessons. Lessons of standing in trust, releasing control and manipulation, opening to new possibilities and insights, letting go of blame and judgment and going with the flow of knowing that God knows exactly what He is doing. Refuse to be a controller—attempting to control the uncontrollable (other people and events). Don't resist chaos, but rather coming to understand its benefits. For what you resist, persists. Resist chaos and all you get is more chaos.

Remember, it is always, "Yea, though I walk *through* the valley of the shadow of death." *Through*, not "pitch your tent and stay there." It is not a camping ground. Therefore, in the midst of upheaval and uncertainty, we have the opportunity to practice trust in the ever-transforming power of God. When we can truly do this, our lives become deeper and more enriched. Painters, writers and musicians have long known that creativity blossoms when they embrace chaos. They strive for that magical moment when they lose control and their art takes on a life of its own.

Some of you may be undergoing life changes, such as going through the death of a loved one, a divorce, a period of self doubt and self questioning, or maybe just a dilemma of some kind. Or you may be going through spiritual chaos often called "the dark night of the soul." All of these can be very frustrating or even painful.

But remember, all pain is born out of resistance. Wherever there is pain, whether it is physical, emotional or spiritual, you can be sure that there is resistance behind it. The way to be free of the pain is to let go of the resistance. When we let go, often, it is those exact experiences that bring us a keener sense of our authentic selves, a deeper level of spirituality, and put us on a new and better path in life.

So how do you let go? When Jesus was on the cross, he said, "Father, into thy hands I commend my Spirit." For you, it can be as simple as, "Father I give this over to you." Letting go happens when you focus less on trying to make things happen, less on being attached to any particular outcome. When you give your circumstance to God, you no longer put your trust in people, you trust that there is a Higher Order taking place. You put your trust in God.

Then things will start to fall into place. Synchronicities will happen. When life seems to be at its most complicated is when you need to let go of your resistance so the underlying order can emerge. Let go of the struggle and you will see that there is a Divine Intelligence at work at all times and in all places. Marcus Bach once wrote, "Life, I have decided, is so constructed, and in such order, that happenings that you didn't expect to happen are actually things that are supposed to happen."

I read a wonderful story not long ago, a story of letting go so the Divine Plan could unfold. A woman lived in chronic chaos of long standing, for she ached from a broken heart, which had been broken many years ago. Her pain and misery prevented her from participating in life. Her friends kept telling her that she needed to get out and date, but she refused.

One night the woman realized that this was no way to live. She needed to let go and let God in. She asked the Holy Spirit to purify her perceptions. The woman was then inspired to give internet dating a try. She started chatting online with a man and at one point she asked, "Where do you live?"

"Seventeenth and Dahlia."

"I live at Seventeenth and Dahlia."

"Really! What building?"

"I live at 4670 Dahlia."

"I live at 4670 Dahlia. What apartment number?"

"I live at number twelve."

"You're kidding! I live at number 13."

So the man and the woman walked out of their respective apartments and met each other face-to-face. They dated for about a year and just recently got married.

You see, when you are in resistance you can't see what is right in front of you. When you let go, you can see how God meticulously places people, situations and events in your path for your highest good. There is a Divine capacity within you that causes right connections, which in turn will lead you to the proper sequence in the unfoldment of your daily affairs. There is a Divine pattern, a mission and a purpose for each of us. Don't ever think that you have been left out. God has you especially in mind.

Many times we may need a period of chaos to shift us into what is really meant to happen. At first it may seem we are guided to people or situations that do not match our expectations. But there is a natural order to all things, which reveals itself in apparent chance encounters that are cosmically orchestrated—synchronicities. Synchronicities unite you with experiences in a way that cannot be described by a linear explanation. Forces come together in time and in space to provide just what is needed. The effect of these forces is to trigger your awareness that there is something greater going on here. That there is a Higher Purpose at work.

So if you are in that place where you have been living in the same old withered tree and a whirlwind has just swept it away, get ready! For something truly spectacular awaits you just around the corner.

21.

The Synergy of Divine Order

Have you ever found yourself walking down the street, flowers in bloom everywhere, the sun shining brightly, not a cloud in the sky, the world fresh with the promise of new life, yet you don't see any of the loveliness—your mind is preoccupied with worry and fear?

When you are caught up in worries, you are effectively absent from the life all around you.

My dad has often been known as a world class worrier, to the point that if I had a pimple on my forehead when I was growing up, he would worry that it might invade the nerves of my brain. He worried so much that he got an ulcer. It is said that fully 75 percent of all doctors' visits are due to worry-related disorders. A friend of mine even worries whenever she has a little discomfort in her stomach, saying, "I wonder if it's a brain tumor." Excuse me?! What does your stomach have to do with your brain?

We worry about our bodies, we worry about our jobs, we worry about our future, we even lay in bed worrying about possibly having said the wrong thing to a friend, again! We ask worrisome questions of ourselves, such as, "I know I want to do something more, something different but what?" or "What should I do with my life? Where should I go? What's next?"

When we ask these kinds of questions, we may feel as if God is nowhere to be found, yet that is not so. For myself, I turn to the idea that God is always working on my behalf. Know for yourself, that God right now is working on your behalf, bringing everything into place for your highest good.

There are two little words that will assist you mightily during worrisome times. These two little words woven into human thought can make the difference between failure and success. When united, they are among the greatest words in the English language. They are vision words, action words. They are words I strongly suggest that you declare on an everyday basis.

These words are "Divine Order."

Divine Order is both a spiritual law and a spiritual faculty. In declaring Divine Order, you can achieve remarkable results. Divine Order isn't a technique, a special gift for the privileged few, or a matter of intellectual advantage. It is a very real, very powerful spiritual faculty which every person has. When you begin to exercise Divine Order, you will witness miracles of always being in the right place at the right time.

So what is Divine Order? It is the capacity in you that causes right connections. It leads you to the proper sequence in the unfoldment of your mind, your body and affairs. Divine Order creates synergy.

Sometimes people live in this synergy without even knowing it. For example, a soon-to-be young bride was boating with her fiancé. She let her hand trail in the water—only to lose her engagement ring. Twenty years later, her husband and children caught a seven-pound trout in the same lake. As they were cleaning the fish, lo and behold, there was the ring in the fish's belly!

Divine Order is the grace of God that brings to us exactly what we need, exactly when we need it. It is being in the right place at the right time. With Divine Order working on your behalf, there is nothing to worry about. When we work with the law of Divine Order, much of what it can do appears to us as magical or miraculous. We cannot necessarily see Divine Order in our lives when we declare it, for it first works in the spiritual realm and under spiritual law.

Now there are times when we choose not to exercise our Divine Order faculty, and we resort to other ways and means of doing things, such as using a negative approach to try to get things done. We worry, we fuss, we put things off, and we labor over unimportant things. The other day as I was worrying about something, I got a telephone call. When I hung up, I thought, "Now what was I worrying about?" I wanted to get back to whatever I was worrying about!

When we worry or take a negative approach, we soon get our minds, bodies and affairs in a state of wrong connections or improper sequence, a condition is generally known as disorder. As a friend of mine likes to say, "Disorder is unattractive under all circumstances." But perhaps one of the most undesirable aspects of disorder is the feeling of being out of control. When you worry, it may feel like you are in control, but you are not. You are out of control, because you have forgotten God.

So many of our disorders can be prevented or corrected if we learn to quicken and utilize Divine Order. We need to ask ourselves, "Do we believe more in our worry or in the Divine working things out for our good?" Declaring Divine Order is saying that you completely trust in God to take care of everything. Believe it or not there is a Higher Order than your worry-based order! When we declare and know that there is Divine Order coming out of every situation, things always seem to fall into place—no matter how disruptive they may seem at the time.

Whenever challenges arise in your life, firmly and faithfully declare Divine Order, *"I affirm Divine Order, and all parts of my life fall into place easily. Everything I need comes to me in Divine right timing. All is well in my life; I am truly blessed."* This affirmation will readjust you and set you in perfect alignment with the law of Divine Order, so that God's harmonizing presence can reign supreme in you and in your world.

A young man approached a logging crew foreman, and asked for a job. "That depends," replied the foreman, "Let's see you chop down this tree." The young man stepped forward and skillfully chopped down a great tree. Impressed, the foreman exclaimed, "You can start Monday!" Monday, Tuesday, Wednesday and Thursday rolled by. Thursday afternoon the foreman told the young man, "You can pick up your pay check on the way out today." Startled, the young man replied, "I thought you paid on Fridays." "Normally we do," said the foreman. "But we're letting you go today because you've fallen behind. Our daily charts show that you've dropped from first place on Monday to last place today." "But I'm a hard worker," the young man objected, "I arrive first, leave last and have even worked through my coffee breaks!" The foreman, sensing the young man's integrity, thought for a minute, and then asked, "Have you been sharpening your axe?" The young man replied, "No sir, I've been working too hard to take the time for that!"

There's nothing wrong with activity and hard work, but God doesn't want us to get so busy that we neglect to bring in God's harmonizing power. If you don't take time to sharpen your axe, your life may become unmanageable and chaotic. Take time on a daily basis to firmly and faithfully declare Divine Order. This is your way of letting God's peace and active harmony become a living, constant and lasting part of your life. It is then that right connections are made and proper sequence then begins to occur.

Years ago, one of my congregants had endured a very frustrating marriage. Her husband finally walked out and left her penniless. Now, the woman understood the idea of Divine Order, so she declared Divine Order in her life every day. In a short period of time, the woman bumped into an acquaintance who knew of her ability to give good parties. The acquaintance asked if she would be interested in catering a party. She did such a great job of it, that others at this party hired her, and now she has a very successful catering company. Not only that, she crossed paths with a old high school flame and they are now happily married. The woman said to me, "Through declaring these two little words of faith, God's good has come to me in wise and wonderful ways. It almost seems like magic!" She proved that it pays to take a positive step in faith and declare Divine Order, because it will always lead you to something better.

What is it that brings such welcome manifestations and improvement into our lives? In Unity we believe that when your word of Truth quickens your faculty of Divine Order, the power of your declaration projects itself as a spiritual force into whatever needs its beneficial impact. Wherever it goes, it immediately erases any wrong connection and establishes a right one. Often, this is done as quick as a flash. The work begins in a realm beyond our present limitations, in the spiritual realm of our existence. Because Divine Order is a spiritual faculty, the way it works is spiritual and the work it accomplishes is spiritual.

Put your Spirit and life in order by replacing fearful, doubt-ful, angry thoughts with thoughts of God's order. Everyday, before you even get out of bed, declare Divine Order and you will see right and satisfying connections reveal themselves to you in beautiful ways. Accept God's order, His purpose, His plan, and His will for you, and you will see the blessed orderly development of your life and affairs.

Thus you will have let God's peace and active harmony become a wonderful constant in your life.

22.

Breast Cancer 101

My experience with breast cancer was actually—surprisingly—a positive one.

Of course, when I first received the diagnosis I was devastated. I believed that I had lost my faith. Being a Minister, that wasn't a very comforting place.

When I shared with friends and family that I had lost my faith, they immediately got on the phone to prayer groups and friends to have them pray for me. Within 24 hours, I was on prayer lists all over the world. It was amazing how very aware I was of those prayers. Needless to say, my faith came back stronger than ever. My spirits were very high. As I entered the hospital for surgery, the nurses, doctors and technicians were amazed at how positive and joyous I was. Not to mention, how quickly I healed and recovered. It was the most spiritual experience of my life.

You see, prayer changes things. It changes the very frequencies of our bodies, our minds and our lives. For example, Dr. Larry Dossey, internist and chief of staff at a major Dallas hospital, found much to his surprise that a carefully controlled study showed that cardiac patients who were prayed for daily did better on average than patients not receiving prayers. This, despite that neither the nearly 400 patients studied, their doctors or nurses knew who was being prayed for and who wasn't. Similarly, Yale University research of 3,000 elderly patients found that people who prayed on a daily basis had strokes half as frequently as those who rarely or never prayed. Dr. Dossey was so intrigued by these studies, that he continued to investigate such phenomena, resulting in his highly regarded book, *Healing Words*.

To me, that says that there is a lot more to prayer than we can possibly know.

If you or a loved one struggles with a challenging diagnosis, I strongly suggest that you call good friends and family members and ask them to put you on their prayer lists, and to call as many other prayer lists as possible. Let them know your date and time of surgery or other treatments. Have them pray for the doctors and nurses as well as for your well-being.

For the God to whom we pray is the presence of love, waiting to be called on. The key is to *call* on Him. We must ask to receive. With that, God makes His presence available for every woman, man and child.

Pray! Ask for what you need and want. God hears, always.

Some online prayer resources are:

Positive Christianity
http://www.positivechristianity.org/request.htm

Silent Unity
https://www.unity.org/prayer/request-prayer
800-669-7729

Center for Spiritual Living
http://csl.org/en/make-a-prayer-request

Jonnie Coleman's Prayer Service
https://cutemple.org/?page_id=1237
773-568-1717

The Wailing Wall in Jerusalem
http://free.messianicbible.com/enter-prayer-wall/

Little Darklings

The other day I was chatting with a friend who said, "Have you ever noticed that there are people who love nothing more than to drag you down?" Hmm. I haven't experienced that in a very long time, and I'll tell you why.

I have found that there are two ways to be sure such individuals don't affect you. First, recognize when you come across what I call "little darklings," those depressing thoughts of despair, fear or blame that lurk in our consciousness, but which only people who thrive on negativity seek to share. Once recognized, you can refuse to take part in such people's darkness. Because you see, little darklings need attention to feed off and grow. These misery-making thoughts have no entrance into your life unless you engage them.

Secondly, start your day in a positive way. Pump yourself up with positive energy so that no negativity can even come close to you. Declare your affirmations. Listen to upbeat music or remember times that made you profoundly happy. Or talk to a dear friend who keeps you on a positive path.

Begin today, this very moment, to come awake and refuse, actively, to spend one more moment of your life lending your precious life force to a little darkling's negative purpose. Revel in a positive and happy way to live!

23.

—∞∞∞—

Accept Change

Every day I'm getting a little older. So are you. Even now, right this minute, you are older than when you first woke up this morning. At times, getting older can be pretty subtle—a few crow's feet, a couple of wrinkles. Other times, not so much—your hair turns gray or you find stray hairs on your pillow in the morning. Or you may even find hair growing in places on your face where you never knew hair could grow. You gain weight or you lose weight. Knees creak, bending over becomes a challenge.

Then there are the other, more pernicious, symptoms of getting older. Like when one of the family's teenagers comes up to you and says, "You know, I'd like to get 'Toad the Wet Sprocket' and 'Nine inch Nails'." You get all excited because you think the teen wants supplies from the hardware store. Finally, some DIY initiative—only to find out that your teen is referring to their favorite musical groups.

Or you go to your doctor for your annual check up and the nurse asks, "How old are you?" You tell the nurse your age and the nurse says, "Oh, really? People your age usually experience hypertension, diabetes and arthritis. How many of those symptoms do you suffer from?"

Personally I don't like it. I don't want it. In fact, I'm not sure it plays any particular part in God's over-all vision of good for us. Getting older makes no sense to me and yet, there is absolutely nothing we can do about it. Here's the thing, like it or not, change happens. It is an inevitable part of our human experience. Everything that exists is in a constant state of change. Everything in nature, all of creation changes eternally because everything is energy, and energy is always in the process of transformation.

We have witnessed tremendous changes in the world around us, many due to the influence of technology—which impact our lifestyles, yes, but also how we view ourselves. Our assumptions about who we are and how we relate to our world are being challenged if not shattered. Change is all around us. Yet very few of us have learned how to deal with change in a healthy or graceful way.

We fear and resist change. A part of us wants to cling stubbornly to the old and the familiar. Yet no matter how comfortable the "old" is for a while, eventually it gets very uncomfortable. It is as if God is pushing us out of the nest. Sometimes we find ourselves pushed out of the nest when a loved one dies, or a divorce happens, or a job changes, a move occurs, or we let go of a belief system. At the time, such triggering events may feel like a crisis. But remember this, crisis precedes transformation.

One of the definitions of crisis is "a crucial turning point." The very word "crisis" is derived from the Greek word meaning, "to decide." Each crisis can be a turning point that leads to the death of an old way and the birth of a new life. When you are faced with a crisis, I rejoice with you, because it means that God's plan is trying to push through to something better on the other side.

A number of years of ago, I counseled a woman who was in her late 40s. She had been married for 25. She never had a job out in the world. She'd devoted her life to raising her family and promoting her husband. She always felt like something was wrong in her marriage, yet she couldn't put her finger on it. Only now that her children were raised, did she finally have the time and mental space to reflect on what could be wrong. When the woman came to me, she was in a state of crisis. She was confused about what to do.

I suggested that the woman set a bedtime intention. "Ask God for clarity," I told her, "whether it comes in the form of your dreams or a strong impulse, be open to how it comes to you. Whatever you do, just let go and let God do His work." That very night the woman dreamed that her husband had been having a whole other life with a woman across town, with whom he also had children. And that his double life had been going on for years.

The next morning, she woke up and told her husband about the dream, at which point he confessed. Her dream gave her the information she needed, which allowed her to make the choice to leave her husband.

She was being pushed out of the nest. Bear in mind, the

woman had never worked outside of the home before. She had to learn a whole new way of life. She decided to start her own company that would give seminars to help women in transition. Because of her willingness to accept the crisis as an opportunity to change for the better, the woman became very successful, both in her professional and personal life.

If you are in crisis, God is asking you to change. To live is to grow, to grow is to change, to change is to die to the old. And to die to the old brings about something better. But we resist change. We hear with "fear muffs" on our ears. We hear with our broken hearts, our shattered egos, or with our anger. We want to stay exactly where we are. Yet to fear change is to fear life itself. To be fully alive we must be willing to be changed, to surrender to the moment without resistance. That can be hard to do.

Toltec mythology tells us that the angel of death is always beside us, ready to take everything away from us. Everything belongs to the angel of death; nothing is ours to keep, including our physical body. Knowing this, we surrender to the angel of death and accept the transformation of life. But the Toltecs also believe that for everything that the angel of death takes away, life gives us something new and better. If we become too attached to what is taken away, we cannot receive the gifts of life.

We need to surrender, to accept change, to be in a place of non-resistance. To surrender fully means to let go of our attachment to how we think things should be, to let go of the anger, frustration and resistance. It doesn't mean being a door-mat. It means surrendering to a Higher plan. When we do this, we experience life with less grasping, less attachment, and less suffering.

Ecclesiastes 3:1 states, "There is a time for everything, and a season for every activity under the sun." There is a time for surrendering, especially when things don't look the way you think they should look. For example, a snowstorm blew out the power at a friend's house. She was complaining about the lack of electricity to some other friends until finally she said something very wise, "So I guess all I can do is surrender." In that moment, her electricity came back on. Her take-away? "Surrender is like magic!" Indeed, it is.

When you surrender your frustration, your anger, your resistance, then the Divine plan God has for you naturally unfolds. It is rarely stated in words, but it can be found by simply looking at what is in front of us. Step-by-step, day-by-day, God's plan is displayed before our eyes. When we trust that God knows exactly what He is doing, when we surrender to Him, we see God's plan in concrete experiences that lead us to where we need to be at precisely the right time. God has a future for us that is God's business, not our business. We don't have to worry about it.

If you are not happy with your life's adventure at present, take inventory of all your attachments. Where do feel you have to be right? Where are you stuck and feel that there is no way out? What are some of the feelings you are hanging on to, such as resentment, anger or unforgiveness? Are there judgments you are unwilling to release? Do you insist that a situation must turn out a certain way?

Let go! Make a new start. Live a life that is young, vital and alive—at any age.

24.

∽∞∽

If Not Now, When?

"I will love this day as if it is my last. And if it is my last, it will be my greatest monument. This day, I will make the best of my life. This day, I will drink every minute to its fullest. I will savor its taste and give thanks. I will make each hour count and each minute I will trade only for something of value."—Og Mandino, *The Greatest Salesman in the World*.

When you and I live our lives in the way Og Mandino describes, something wonderful happens, a power emerges within us that lifts us out of the ordinary. Strange as it may seem, this power can transform your life so thoroughly, so radically, so completely, that as it does your own family may look at you and say, "What's wrong with you?"

Even though we may not realize it, that power is the power of awareness, available to us in this now moment. Awareness is a higher state in which your whole being feels and understands the extraordinariness of the present moment. As you become aware, you will start to really live. As Oscar Wilde said, "To live is the rarest thing in the world. Most people exist, that is all."

It often amazes me that we have not yet learned how to truly live our lives. We tend to let our lives happen to us from the outside. We drift and wonder, at times complaining and cursing our lives. But the Universal order of things is that all happens first "within" and then "without." The Universal order of things starts with our being. We've been given this great Spirit of life which is God's own Spirit within us, but for the most part we don't love it or we are not aware of it.

We may say, "Well, I'll think about that manana, tomorrow. Or when I get such and such done, or when things get good." And I say, "Not tomorrow, but today. This is the only day you've got!" If this were your last day, would you want to spend it in anger, jealousy or in trying to control other people? It has been said that our lives are God's gift to us, but that what we do with our lives, is our gift to God.

Our job is to be present with Him in this moment, in every moment. If we aren't, we go out into our day just as a human being, subject to all the trials and tribulations of the human world, without Divine guidance. There is no God sitting up in the sky, looking down upon you and judging your actions, but there is a God center within you that knows everything you do and knows everything you need. If you tune into the moment, you will see that you stand on holy ground, because God is right here where you are, available to you this very minute.

Take time, right now, to savor your moment. According to Webster's Dictionary, the definition of savor is, "to give one's self to the enjoyment of the moment." The fourth chapter of Philippians states, "Always be full of joy in the Lord." When you savor the moment, you can feel the element of joy, you can feel the presence of God.

What if we were full of joy, not just sometimes, but all the time? That may seem like such a strange statement, living in this world as we do, but I believe that it is possible to be full of joy all the time, even if I'm not always allowing myself to be so. The truth is, whether the circumstances in our lives are good or bad, we can choose with our thoughts to be miserable about them or to find something to savor in a moment.

Sometimes we do not savor the moment but live in fear. Instead of being present with God, we entertain our fears. When we do that, we miss out on the beauty and the abundance of the moment. It is truly not a God-centered place to be. In the late 80s, for example, I read a book describing imminent worldwide calamities and disasters. Motivated by fear, I read everything on survival. I also got some dear friends involved in my fear, some of whom figured it would be a good idea to purchase underground bunkers.

Then one day I had a couple of realizations:

1. I had sold my faith out to fear. I was so involved in protecting myself from a dreaded future, that I was ignoring all the joy available in the present moment.
2. The predictions made in the book did not come to pass.

I decided there had to be more to life than living in fear. Have there been calamities and disasters? Certainly, there always have been, and it seems that our world is such that there will continue to be frightening events. But fear keeps us from what is real in the moment and living in the moment is living life in Spirit.

I love watching people take pictures on their phones—of their latte, their pets, their shoes, selfies. They document everything. We would do well to be aware of our lives with such detail! By taking a moment to step back, become more aware as we observe our lives, we can assimilate a bit of beauty, a slice of bliss, and a feeling of pure joy. Just one moment in which to be aware. I know this seems like a simple concept, but actually doing it is another thing.

When I first put this concept into practice, I decided to deliberately take pleasure in even the smallest moment. I repeated an affirmation to myself, "I am savoring this moment." All day long I kept savoring the moment. I was wonderfully blissed out. The test came when I received a call that took me off course. I found myself reacting to an unpleasant situation. Then I wondered, "Can I savor this moment?" Sure enough, I was able to step out of reacting and see how things were unfolding in a natural way. At that point, I realized that when we live our lives being aware of the present moment, there really is a power that lifts us out of the ordinary of our lives into the extraordinary of Spirit.

It was truly a wonderful lesson for me, one that I try to live as much as I possibly can. Living from that place means being able to encounter the Sacred. You can find the Sacred in a cup of tea, in a chat with a stranger or in a hug from a friend. Stopping to notice the Sacred in these moments encourages more of the Sacred in our lives.

We lose a lot of the good that life has to offer by simply not letting it in. We subconsciously say "Uh-huh," without really paying attention to what just happened. Often we take something wonderful for granted. Or we are doing so many things at once, that none of them get our attention. If we do not remind ourselves to take in a particular encounter or sensation, to be fully aware, we may go through the motions without allowing the experience to imprint and enrich us.

Make it a practice to stop every so often simply to be present to the moment. Notice what you see, what you smell, who is with you, how this moment feels emotionally and physically. With that, you will be well on your way to maximum joy from your life.

The practice of stopping is especially important during major turning points such as reunions, special trips and celebrations. These are events we want to experience thoroughly, but we risk losing because they so often take place when many other things are going on around them. In the Jewish tradition, there is a wedding custom that allows the bride and groom 15 minutes alone immediately following the ceremony to take in what just happened—so they might savor that unique and wonderful moment. What a precious use of time!

In the midst of whatever is happening, take a "savoring" break every so often. Help yourself be fully aware by saying, "I am savoring this moment." When you do, something wonderful will happen. You will be lifted by the power of awareness out of your ordinary day. You will experience the Sacred.

I guarantee it!

25.

Inspired Decisions

When I was a teenager, my mom would come into my room every day and exclaim, in a cheerful singsong voice, "Gooood Moooorning! Isn't it a beautiful mooooorning! Isn't it a great day to be haaaaappy!" Every. Single. Morning. It was very annoying.

When you're a teenager with hormones raging and trying to figure out who you are in life, sometimes you're not feeling the joy. I remember telling her, "Mom, I'm not feeling so happy." "Well, you can deciiiiiide if you want to be haaaaappy," she'd singsong back. Argh! My mom still sings like that in the morning. The difference is—I really like it now.

How can we do that? How can we just "decide" to be happy? What is the process of making a decision?

In the fast moving pace of our lives, certainly one of the greatest problems is indecision. Fortunes have been lost, opportunities passed up, chances for happiness slipped by and minds seethed through restless nights because a decision needed to be made, "Which way should I go? Should I buy or sell? Should I take this job or that one? Should I move or stay put?" Life demands that you make decisions about many things every day. Some are of little importance, but others can affect the course of your entire life. Yet sometimes, we are stuck at the fork in the road, unable to make a decision.

Indecisiveness is caused by fear. It is this fear that leads to procrastination. We are afraid to make the wrong move, do the wrong thing or say the wrong word. We are afraid to make the wrong choice. This anxious concern is what motivates a person to consult with family, friends, work associates, tarot card readers, palm readers, astrologers and others. Indeed, there may be times when asking others for advice could be useful, but when it comes to making decisions or choosing the right path, all the advice from everyone may not seem to help at all. In fact, it might confuse us even more.

My friend, Chris Chenoweth (http://www.positivechristianity.org/inforev.htm), told me a story once about Norman Vincent Peale, author of *The Power of Positive Thinking*. Dr. Peale was sitting on an airplane next to a young woman who struck up a conversation with him. When she discovered who she was talking to, she asked him for help in making a decision, "Dr. Peale, I have been dating two men. Both of them have proposed to me. I'm not sure which one to say 'yes' to. Can you give me some advice?" "Sure," replied Dr. Peale, "I don't think you should marry either of them." "Why is that?" she asked. "If you have to ask who to marry," Dr. Peale said, "You're not in love with either one of them." Indeed, his words rang true for her.

You see, all the answers you could ever need abide at the core of your being. The greatest service any therapist, teacher, astrologer or counselor can offer you is to remind you of what you already know, just as Dr. Peale did—of what rings true for you.

It's what happens when someone says something that resonates with you, and you say, "That's it! That's it!"

But why does one piece of advice move you more than others? Because you already know the answer. This was just outward validation that matched your inner knowing. When something is right for you, you know it. When something is not right for you, you know it. Your job is to get in touch with your inner knowing, your inner wisdom.

Your inner wisdom is always speaking to you, 24 hours a day. Decisions are not so much to be made as they are to be discovered. All you need to remember is this one thing: that you are in the presence of God, also known as Divine Intelligence or Divine Wisdom, in which you live and move and have your being. Right now, you are in pure Divine Intelligence. You are totally connected with Divine Wisdom.

When you think that, your mind is separate and alone. You will definitely feel the pressure of having to make a decision, because you have nothing else to work with other than your own human knowledge and experience. Your human ego. It is then that we tend to make decisions that are not of our highest good. But if you live from the Divine Intelligence of God, there is always a right answer, for there is always that in you that is The Knower; the God-part of you that knows what to do, where to be and where to go at all times. In Isaiah 65:24 it states, "Before they call, I will answer."

One of my favorite stories is of a colleague, who had been dating a woman in Texas for a few years. She now wanted him to marry her. He asked everyone for advice. Some people told him, "Yes! Marry her!" Others said, "No way!" He became very confused. One day, when he was out driving, he asked God for a sign as to what to do. Any sign! At that moment, a semi-truck pulled out in front of him with a bumper sticker that read, "Don't Mess With Texas." That resonated with him! It felt true for him. He had his answer—she wasn't the right bride for him.

Ralph Waldo Emerson knew of this when he said, "There is guidance for each of us, and by lowly listening we shall hear the right word." Our guidance often comes in the form of an intuitive flash, which in Unity we define simply as inner knowing filtering through an unblocked mind. We have all had intuitive flashes; the problem is that we do not always have confidence in those flashes. We do not trust the action of Divine Mind. Think back to a time when you had to make a decision—how you pondered and probed your mind in an anxious and frustrating attempt to make the right choice. Recall how suddenly, you had an intuitive flash of a direction, but turned away from it because it looked unrealistic or impossible. Later you realized that the intuitive sense of direction you turned away from was the right choice you should have made instantly.

Your guidance is always present. You cannot really make a wrong choice. If you do make a choice that is not for your highest good, Divine Intelligence will again lead you to where you need to be. There is no reason to be afraid of making a decision, because any step you take will eventually bring you to your good. It's the nature of our connection to Divine Wisdom. It is the way we are wired.

Here is a proven technique to help you make inspired decisions:

1. Let your mind become an *instrument* of Divine Intelligence rather than the *source* of your decisions. Trying to squeeze a decision out of your human mind will only block the flow of the right answer. Relax and center yourself in peace.

2. Realize that God knows, and God is in you. Therefore, you know. Acknowledge that you really don't have to make a decision at all, that on another level, the decision has already been made. All you have to do is feel what resonates with you.

3. Refrain from discussing your concern with other people, as it may interfere with your guidance. Keep the matter to yourself for a while, and be conscious of what rings true for you.

4. Put your concern out of your mind and affirm, "While I sleep, or walk, or work, Divine Intelligence is active on my behalf." Have faith that your words and choices are formed by a transcendent wisdom that is Divinely inspired and Divinely empowered.

If fear comes creeping in, set your concern aside for an "incubation" period. Take a nap, or go for a walk, read or watch television. Be patient. Guidance will come to you and you will feel the truth of it when it does.

Remember, what happens in this process is that you don't make the decision, the decision actually makes you. The answer to your concern exists in God-mind even before you are aware of the need for it, "Before they call, I will answer." With these steps, you can make decisions easily, and they will be the right ones for you!

26.

Assumptions or the Grace of God: Your Choice

One day, I was grocery shopping when, in the dairy section, I bumped into a friend I had not seen in quite some time. I was so excited to see her! Yet, as we were talking, I noticed that her breath was less than desirable.

Oh come on—like you've never been in that kind of situation before?

I wasn't sure whether to tell her or offer her some gum, but it got to the point where I could hardly stand it. So I backed up slightly, only to back right into a big open barrel of cheese. I laughed and said, "Thank God, it was the cheese that smelled! I thought it was you!" She burst out laughing in turn and said, "I thought it was you!"

You see, even though we may think we have all the facts

and we would swear they were the absolute truth, we actually tend to make assumptions about many things. Then we often go on to create a lot of emotional poison as we gossip about our assumptions, or get caught up in the assumptions of others.

Assumptions are a type of judgment, where you see only what you want to see and hear only what you want to hear. You don't perceive things the way they are. It becomes a habit. We make things up which have no basis in reality. Assumptions have only the substance you give them in your mind. So as long as you accept assumptions at their face value, they become very real, and somewhere along the line you will suffer the consequences.

There is a reason why Jesus said, "Judge not according to appearances but judge righteous judgment." Righteous judgment is where you rise above the so-called facts and get more information. For example, in relationships, we assume that our partners know what we want, or at least they *should* know what we want. But when they don't behave in the way we want them to, we get hurt and upset, and then we are full of blame.

Think about it. When was the last time you made an assumption about your loved one? We make all sorts of assumptions because we don't ask questions. We don't ask for enough data. We need to ask for information and to be willing to ask for what we want.

Jesus gave us a good lesson about how we are too quick to assume. In one of his parables, Jesus talks about an unfortunate traveler who became a victim to roadway thieves. The traveler was beaten and stripped of all his possessions, which included his clothes and he was left half dead in a ditch by the side of the road. A priest came by, saw the body, assumed that the man had been drinking too much and passed right on by. After that, a Levite came by with other negative assumptions about the man, which made him unwilling to help. He too passed by.

Then an ordinary person came along, a Samaritan on a business journey. When he saw the traveler in trouble, the Samaritan crossed the road, not to walk by, but to help. Very compassionately, the Samaritan poured oil and wine on the man's wounds, bound him up and took him to an inn. The Samaritan watched over the stranger all night, and in the morning made a generous arrangement for the traveler's continued care.

In the Bible, when Jesus is finished telling his story, he asks, "Who then of these three was the neighbor?" He goes on to say, "The neighbor is the one who had mercy. Go and do likewise." The neighbor is the one who does not assume or judge but rather acts from loving kindness. Go and do likewise as Jesus instructs us.

We cannot experience God at the same time as we are judging. It just doesn't work. In your mind you have the choice of whether or not you want to participate in judgment or to experience more of God. Many times, you will be persuaded to engage in the assumptions and judgments of others and when you do, you know that it doesn't feel good or right. It is a type of separation from God that is called "againstness." It occurs when we feel against a fellow brother or sister.

Get honest with yourself. Check in to see when or with whom you have practiced this kind of separation. Believe it or not, we all have training in separation. We have all had, and probably will continue to have, opportunities where we will be tempted to consider somebody else separate from ourselves.

Opportunities to consider ourselves separate from others abound in every single presidential or political campaign, to name just one example.

The judgments people have about each other for believing on way or another astound me. Much to my dismay, I have noticed that I am not exempt from this behavior. However, the result of assuming or judging in this manner too often results in misplaced anger or resentment. How then can we experience God when we cannot see the God in others? Remember, the same God that is in you is the same God that is in everyone else.

When you hold on to making someone else wrong with your assumptions you live a very limited life. It keeps you and the other person hostage. Lowell Fillmore, in his book *New Ways to Solve Old Problems*, wrote, "Negative judgments obscure the Kingdom of Heaven from our view."

Whenever we hold an assumption or judgment of another we cut ourselves off from the Source, from God. Not only that, but there are often steep prices to pay, in the form of loss of friendship, divorce, unhappy feelings, not to mention the waste of time and energy.

How often have we assumed or judged another person's behavior only to learn later that they were in great pain of some sort? My former husband was diagnosed with multiple sclerosis a year after we were married. Sometimes he would lose his balance when we were walking down the street. I could hear people say, "Look at that man. He is so drunk, his wife has to hold him up." It felt terrible to hear such judgment about him, when I knew the truth of his stumbling.

A good question to ask yourself might be, "Shall I bless or

be less?" Shall we bless our relationships by taking the opportunity to find out the facts, and honor them by listening? Or do we choose to be less than God intended us to be by sitting in judgment?

Many times we assume that everyone sees life the way we do. That others think the way we think and feel the way we feel. This is one of the biggest mistakes we make. Being in the ministry I am quite used to people making assumptions about me. Some of them are downright funny. One time I went on vacation, only to find out on my return that a number of people in the congregation thought I had gotten secretly married.

People make incorrect assumptions about you, too. Believe me, they do it all the time. Yet what may seem like fact to another is not always real. This lesson was driven home to me shortly after the horrific events of September 11, 2001. I was at the airport on my way to Unity Village for a meeting. I knew I would be there for almost a week, so I brought my own snacks, among which were half a loaf of bread, a jar of almond butter, and a little plastic knife. As I was checking my baggage, I was asked to step aside and wait while my luggage was x-rayed.

After a while, my name was called, and I was escorted by a police officer into a little room. There on the screen was my almond butter and my little plastic knife—which to airport security—looked like a real knife and a bomb! The officer swiped my luggage with a piece of material, put the material in the computer, and the computer reported that I had bomb residue on my bag! I said, "I swear, it is only almond butter."

I opened my bag, showed them the almond butter and the knife, and then the officers proceeded to look through every nook and cranny of my luggage. They took another little piece of material, swiped my luggage once again, whereupon it turned out that something was wrong with the computer, not with my luggage or its contents. But because of the way it looked to the airport security—thinking that they had all the evidence—assumptions were made on false pretenses.

How many times do we impose our own perceptions on others? How many times are the false perceptions of others being imposed on you? Have you ever thought about not imposing your assumptions? Just imagine a day where you stop making assumptions. A day where you don't make assumptions about your partner or anyone else in your life.

Watch! Your way of communicating will change. You will communicate clearly and cleanly, free of emotional baggage. You will choose not to gossip, because most gossip is based on false evidence. Best of all, your relationships will no longer suffer from conflicts created by mistaken assumptions.

If you want to bring a difficult relationship back into harmony, stop assuming. If you don't understand something, ask questions and gather your data. Now, some of you may think that this is a simple principle, but remember, most of us have been brought up to do the opposite. We would rather be less than to bless.

So what I am asking is that you start asking questions, get appropriate data and stop any conversation where you might be assuming. If you do this, you will experience God in a most profound way. The Bible does not say, "Wait until some future time to find God." It says *now* is the day of salvation. *Now* is the accepted time. This day belongs to God and we should live in that spirit by rising to a level higher than that of our assumptions.

Choose this day who you will serve, your assumptions or the grace of God. Choose to bless!

Condemnation or Compassion?

Once upon a time, there was a little girl named Lizzie. Her kindergarten teacher asked all the children to draw a picture as a gift for their moms on Mother's Day. The teacher pinned them up on a bulletin board in readiness for that special day. But come the time to take her picture off the bulletin board, Lizzie discovered that someone else had taken her picture! She had nothing to take home to her mom.

Miserable, sure that her mom would be terribly disappointed, Lizzie dragged herself home and give her mom the unpleasant news. Instead, her mom smiled at her and said, "What a beautiful picture it must have been for someone to want it so much that they had to take it! Maybe you will grow up to be a great artist." With that, Lizzie smiled, clapped her hands with delight and felt wonderfully empowered.

There are many ways to look at any given event or situation. At one extreme is the perspective of judgment, fear and guilt. At the other extreme is trust, forgiveness and love. Everything is only a matter of our perception, and perception belongs solely to the perceiver. Not everyone is going to see things the same way.

I know that there are experiences that seem hurtful, but remember, it is not the act that hurts, but your interpretation or your perception of the act. Just as you can choose an interpretation or perception that hurts, you can choose one that heals. *A Course in Miracles* states, "I can elect to change all thoughts that hurt."

Every day, you and I have many opportunities to choose between condemnation and compassion. You can make someone's day, especially your own, by finding interpretations and viewpoints that soothe and bring peace to the soul. Enjoy a new way of perceiving!

27.

Love

One of my favorite quotes from Judith Viorst is, "Infatuation is when you think he's as gorgeous as Robert Redford, as pure as Solzhenitsyn, as funny as Woody Allen, as athletic as Jimmy Connors, and as smart as Albert Einstein. Love is when you realize that he is a gorgeous as Woody Allen, as smart as Jimmy Connors, as funny as Solzhenitsyn, as athletic as Albert Einstein, and nothing like Robert Redford in any category, but you'll take him anyway."

As humorous as this may be, it is also the very crux of a relationship—allowing the other person to be who they are, and loving them as they are. Our relationships often determine our happiness or lack of it. The character of our relationships ranges from the heights of bliss to the depths of devastation, and most of us have been privy to both at some point in our lives.

The focus of this chapter is on what we might call our close or intimate relationships—family, friends, spouses or significant others. Relationships of any kind are an ongoing course in love and forgiveness. Many mystics, in fact, have dissuaded their disciples from leading monastic lives, telling them that being in a relationship was a more difficult but quicker path to self-realization than that of the celibate or hermit.

As Ram Dass said, "If you think that you are enlightened, go spend a week with your parents." Relationships are a fast track to self-awakening because they constantly reflect back to us what we most need to work on in ourselves. No matter where you are, relationships are your constant mirror. Relationships represent assignments for learning. In fact, *A Course in Miracles* refers to these relationships as "Laboratories of the Holy Spirit." Teilhard de Chardin, the renowned paleontologist, poet, philosopher and priest, said of relationships that they are "the blood of spiritual evolution."

Love's promise is that if we are willing to see our relationships as teachers, rather than discard or demean them if they disappoint us, they will lead us to greater self-awareness, forgiveness and compassion. We will become stronger and more confident. The ideal, then, is not to *lose* yourself in a relationship, but rather to *find* yourself in a relationship. For there will come a time when your relationship stands before you and says, "I will descend into your dark and shadow sides with you, and come out on the other side. I see it all. I can take it all. I love it all. So let's do the work together."

Years ago, when I was undergoing treatment for breast cancer, the first ones on the scene were my girlfriends. They never left my side. The bond created between us was so strong that we have seen each other through the tough times in our lives and reveled in our joyous times together. We have seen each other's shadow side, we have accepted each other however we were, loved it all and laughed through it all. There is nothing better than to have someone in your life with whom you can be your most awful self, and know they aren't going to kick you out of their life. They will just hold a place for you to process whatever it is you need to process and love you through it.

Such relationships constitute true intimacy, which can be thought of as "into me see." When you allow another to see who you truly are, they reflect back to you all of yourself, which allows you to heal the dark crevices of your soul. In such a relationship, an environment exists in which you can experience the deepest level of safety and relaxation, which encourages and supports your most profound personal growth. It allows you to be strong enough to look in the mirror and say, "Well, this is my stuff. This is something I need to work on within myself." The highest purpose of intimacy, then, is to call forth the Love that is already present in who you are—to love the person looking back at you in the mirror.

In close relationships, we commit to climbing emotional mountains as we embark together on a potentially scary, and yet extremely rewarding, journey. We become willing to ask each other for help, to totally listen and be totally present. We learn to let go of assumptions and expectations, to accept what is, and not take the other person for granted. And sometimes— when it's appropriate—we learn not to take each other quite so seriously. Being in relationship demands a hero's heart. It is a quest, not just a gift. It is a noble undertaking with an often challenging path. Wasn't that what Jesus meant when he said,

"By this all men will know that you are my disciples, if you just have love for one another."

One of the greatest problems in our society is that we put too much emphasis on finding someone who will love us. Our culture focuses too much on being loved and not enough on being a loving person. We focus on "What can I get from this relationship?" rather than on "What can I contribute to this relationship?" Not only that, but more often that not, we expect our relationship to satisfy our every need. We want commitment so that we can be sure that we will forever be taken care of and provided for.

We may even think that commitment is the definition of love. When I was in my 20s, I dated a young man I had known since the third grade. He lived in Illinois and I lived in San Diego at the time. We spent hours on the phone talking about commitment. "What does it mean to be committed to each other?" "What will happen to our lives if we commit to each other?" "Are we capable of committing to each other?" Finally he said, "If we move to Florida, we can be together and be committed." So I packed everything up, drove cross-country and moved to Florida, not knowing a soul there. I set up house for us and waited for his arrival. I never heard from him or saw him ever again. All I know is that he is alive and well.

That experience provided me with some invaluable life lessons. Here is what I have found to be true: no relationship can work if the other partner is the be-all and end-all of your commitment.

There is only one real commitment that any human being can make, and that is the commitment to God and to your own spiritual growth.

Look at relationships as our spiritual teachers, assignments, if you will, part of a vast plan for our enlightenment. It is God's holy blueprint by which each individual soul is led to a greater awareness of self-love. Relationships refine and define who you are. They are blessings in disguise. If we let them, they always lead us back to our true nature, which is love.

For many people, love has become the Holy Grail of our time. People want more of it, suffer from thinking that they are deficient in it, and search for it all of their lives. But the truth is your very nature is love. Love is who you already are. You can't get it from another person, thinking you are undersupplied. Love is ever-present. It lives as you live. Love is the breath of God. It infuses each of us with life and purpose.

Excitement comes from understanding what love truly is, rather than what we insist it must be. Our task is not to seek love, but to find all the barriers we have built against it. We may not find it easy to express love, to be understanding or even to allow others to be themselves. Yet we express the true nature of love when we love those who displease us, who are difficult to get along with or who are irritating.

One of the most helpful ideas we can hold on to is, "The God in me loves the God in you." Your basic need is not to be loved but to love. Love is a verb. It is something that you do, something you share. If there is any aspect of our relationships that is not reflecting love, then we are being called to step up, to love the other and love ourselves in the process.

I was working at a Church with some other Ministers, one of whom would barge in my office while I was counseling people and start talking to me in a very loud voice, practically yelling!

I found her behavior problematic, to say the least, and very disturbing. It became increasingly difficult for me to be at work. I had to ask myself, "What is she here to teach me? What do I need to learn?" The answer came easily, "She is here to teach you to love in the midst of chaos."

With that understanding in mind, I formed a group with some other people who had similar difficulties with her. We established a rule for ourselves; we would not put the Minister down or gossip about her in any way. We would just get together and send her love. What happened then was amazing. The Minister was transformed. She softened and became a delight to be around. Love is powerful. It can melt away almost any difficulty.

If you were to ask, "What is the purpose of love?" The answer would be, "There is no purpose for love, it is its own reward. The more love you give, the more love you receive." As Saint Augustine said, "I am in love with loving."

Love!

28.

Keep Your Love-Light Shining

The love of my life, Steve, and I went to an arts festival in Palm Springs recently. At one of the booths where an older couple was selling their artwork. The woman was reading a well-worn copy of *The Notebook* by Nicholas Sparks. The movie version is one of my favorites. I have watched it repeatedly, and Steve is always so good to watch it with me. Steve asked the husband, "How many times have you had to see that movie?" The man looked at him and smiled, "Quite a number of times. But I would do anything to make the love of my life happy! And watching that movie makes her happy." You could just feel love radiating from him to his wife.

Have you ever been in the company of people who love each other? Their "love vibration" positively radiates from them.

As kids, my brother and I watched old science fiction movies. With the development of atomic power in the 1940s, sci-fi writers and filmmakers let their imaginations run wild. The movie industry started churning out such classics as "Them," in which the monsters were giant ants; "The Amazing Colossal Man," who kept growing and growing until he was 50 feet tall; "The Giant Ba-heeee-moth," a ginormous underwater lizard; "The Beginning of the End," in which enormous grasshoppers wreaked havoc and threatened Chicago. All of these monsters grew as a result of exposure to large doses of radiation.

We laugh at these movies today, but we do know that there can be danger in radiation exposure, just as radiation has been harnessed for good, such as the radiation treatments that help cancer patients or the radiation used in taking X-rays.

As Unity students, we are called to radiate, specifically to radiate love. Others should be able to bask in the glow of the love radiating from your heart. They should feel expanded and greater in your presence. This is not fanciful thinking. It is based on science. Every beat of your heart sends out electromagnetic energy, 360 degrees around you, at the speed of light. We are all immersed in each other's heartbeats. Our hearts constantly communicate with others in our vicinity, whether you are saying anything or not.

Sometimes it seems like we have over-commercialized love, that we use the word to describe everything from pizza to our spouses, such that many have become desensitized to the subject of love. We become indifferent to its meaning. What the world needs now is love, love, love—bla, bla, bla! But with all the conflicts, frustrations, political division and tensions, not to mention wars, we obviously haven't had enough to say about love.

Love holds immense power. The capacity for love is who we truly are, and we conceal it at a terrible cost to the world and to ourselves. It is about time that we take scripture seriously when it states "God is love," and that "Man is created in the image and likeness of God." It must logically follow that man is created in and of love.

Love is your true nature, whether you are conscious of it or not. Love is the very essence of who you are. Love is what the sea is to a fish. It is what you swim in all of your life. Your job is to be in the sea of love, to radiate love, to give love and to have it expressed in your life. As you come from the vibrational frequency of love, you will see others around you begin to change to match you energetically.

A number of years ago, Eric Butterworth, author of *Discover the Power Within You*, talked about having lost his wallet when he was in the army. His wallet contained what was for him, a substantial amount of money but nothing with a useful address on it, since he was living on base. At first, Eric was very angry and mad at the person who picked up his wallet. But after much thought and self-discipline, he decided to give thanks that there'd been no loss in Spirit, and felt impelled to love and bless whoever had his wallet.

Then, one day when Eric went to the Post Exchange, a young man came up to him, saying that although he'd originally intended to keep the money, he found that he couldn't. Not knowing where to find Eric, he followed an impulse to go to the Post Exchange and wait. The relieved young man returned the wallet and left quickly. Eric was infinitely grateful, not just for the return of the money, but because he had gotten in tune with Divine flow, which allowed the Law of Love to work.

When you allow your heart radiation to speak to other hearts, the greatness in others emerges. For example, when someone says something to you that might ordinarily offend you, you have a choice. You can get angry, and in so doing, stop being a radiating center of love. The result is bitterness, hostility and division. But if you understand the Law of Love, then your heart radiation can communicate on a higher level. You can choose to see the offending person as they really are—a child of God—and you can love them as such. The person will feel your love radiation, and in this bright light, negative feelings are then softened, if not entirely forgotten.

Try this experiment while sitting in a crowded room, perhaps at an airport or in an elevator. Pick out someone who looks glum and tense, or unfriendly, and fix your attention on that one person, without letting him/her know you're doing it. Just look and let your love go forth. Let it radiate. Watch the person melt. The person may even have a little smile come over their face. Then, shift your attention to someone else equally unhappy. You can actually transform an entire room when you keep your consciousness high on love. It's fun! Try it.

You probably think I am just sitting here on Sundays during our meditation, but in reality, I am sending love radiation your way!

You see, where love exists, there is joy, peace, friendliness and harmony. Where love is not acknowledged, there is division, fear and frustration. We all live within the Law of Love, but only if we let the Law work *in* us, does it work *for* us. When you act according to the Law of Love, you cease being a part of the division and problems of the world. You become a part of the solution - a peaceful, harmonious society.

People who have had near death experiences, without exception, report that the only thing you get to take with you when you die is love. It is the only thing that matters, the only thing that is real. Money, houses, fame, cars, jewelry—none of those matters—only the love.

Are you allowing love in right now? Are you giving love out right now? It is easy to let love in from those you love, and to give love to those who are loving towards you, but what if your "love radiation" was on all the time? Not just for a selected few. Like the Dalai Lama. He *knows* that he is in and of love like a fish is to water. He knows that he is loved and lovable; his love light is always turned on. People rise to his vibration in his presence, and their greatness emerges in response to that love.

You and I may come to Church each Sunday, and here we may be willing to extend love and receive love with each other. Then the service ends, and on the way home we may stop at a Starbucks. Once there, we probably don't radiate love to the barista. It fact, our heartbeats might communicate indifference. It's like an unspoken societal agreement exists that doesn't let us feel how precious we are to each other on this planet.

But the Dalai Lama and other teachers of high consciousness, like Mother Teresa and Mahatma Gandhi, don't turn their love off. They would go into a Starbucks and see a precious child of God. They would have a heart connection with the barista that they wouldn't hide! Their whole presence says, "Isn't it thrilling to be in each other's heartbeats?" They live in love, so they are in love with their whole experience of being there. They know that God loves the barista, and as they treat others as children of God, they receive even more love in return.

We, on the other hand, allow the outside world to turn our love-light, our love radiation, on and off. We allow the outside world to dictate our emotional well-being. You and I may not be saints (well, at least I'm not!), but that is not reason to avoid the Truth that you live and have your being in love. Just like in those old science fiction movies where radiation made things bigger, your love radiation will change things. It will make hearts expand. It will make the greatness in others emerge. It will heal every hurt and raise the vibration in every environment.

Therefore, you might as well turn on your love-light now, and keep it on! For love is the only thing that is real.

29.

Blessed Are Those Who Love For They Shall Inherit Fulfillment

A t every moment each of us makes a choice between complete and total self-worth or not feeling good enough. In our natural state, we are glorious beings. We know our worth and we know our value. In the world of illusion, we often give our power and our value away to several things—the past, our insecurities and other people or things.

Our past is usually where we hold grudges, resentments, hurt and anger. Our insecurities usually stem from when we lack connection with the Divine. Without a sense of connection, we may hold a belief that we are somehow inadequate and feel a desperate need for things to fill us up. Like "that" relationship, or shopping, or buying a new car, or indulging in food or alcohol. Yet we fail to find fulfillment because we are looking for it in the world of false power.

A story is told of a young Rabbi who lived in a small mountain village. He was a clever young man who believed himself to be very wise and had a great desire to be recognized for his tremendous gifts. He so wanted others to acknowledge his wisdom, but, to his great disappointment, the people of his village never honored or respected him to his satisfaction. This, of course, left him feeling not good enough and resentful.

One day, an old Master, famous for his wisdom, came to the village. The young Rabbi saw this as an opportunity to prove his awesome skills. The old master was going to speak before a gathering of villagers the following morning. The young Rabbi decided to devise a test for the Master that would prove the young Rabbi's excellence.

At the right moment in the middle of the gathering, the young man would approach the Master holding a tiny bird in his hand. Then he would ask the following question, "Master I have a bird in my hand, can you please tell me if the bird is alive or dead?" If the Master answered, "The bird is alive," the young Rabbi could easily crush the small creature and hold it out for all to see, proving the Master was wrong, and therefore not wise. If the Master answered, "The bird is dead," the young Rabbi would simply let the bird fly from his hand. In either case, the young Rabbi would have clearly demonstrated his cleverness and superior wisdom.

The next day when the Master stood in front of the huge crowd of villagers, the young Rabbi stood up and challenged him, "Master, we all know that you are wise and clever, but please, sir, if you will, can you tell me if the bird I hold in my hand is alive or dead?" The Master was silent for a moment. Everyone waited breathless for his response. Then with loving eyes, the Master looked at the young man and gently replied, "It's up to you, my friend, it's up to you."

We hold the key to our self-love. Our worth and value are never decided by people or things outside of ourselves. Seeking the approval of outside people or circumstances only results in our giving our power away. We are ultimately responsible for how we see ourselves. It is up to you, my friend, it is up to you.

Healing of all kinds, physical, emotional or mental comes when we are able to meet ourselves with unconditional appreciation, love, gratefulness and compassion. Love is not something that we extract from the past, or from our relationships, or from outside things. Love is right here, right now, today in this moment, this instant. You are God's child. He loves you very much in every moment of every day. If you are feeling His love right now, then you are claiming your highest glory.

Now, the kind of love that I am talking about is not the kind of love you look for from a spouse, or a family member, or friends. It is the love that already resides within your own spiritual nature. Jesus' most quoted teaching is "Love thy neighbor as thyself." This is surely true, but too often people do not love themselves—which makes it hard to love others fully!

We see this all the time. For example, when we don't draw healthy boundaries for ourselves. When we don't delegate tasks that can be done by others. When we can't say "no." When we don't tell the truth and come clean. When we don't take care of ourselves health-wise. When we put ourselves down. When we compare ourselves to others. Do any of these sound familiar to you? They certainly do to me!

We need to get back to basics. You are a Divine being having a human experience, and the Divine is not insufficient in any way. You have all the love you will ever need within you. Love is the most potent force in the Universe, but it must be called forth from within you. That is your job—to reclaim your inner love. When you do this you set boundaries, you say "no" easily, you reach for vegetables instead of fries and you don't feel the need to compare yourself to others. You feel fulfilled in everything you do.

I remember when I went to my first Church as a Minister. Mind you, I was a mere 23 years old. My Board of Trustees was an all-male board. There were times when they would meet without me and make decisions without me. I didn't take care of myself. I didn't set boundaries. I didn't say "no." I didn't tell the truth about how I really felt. Instead I smoked and ate junk food. Not exactly the picture of self-love and self-nurturing!

I told my mom that the Board was going to meet without me—again. They made sure that I knew that the meeting was closed off to me. They had their reasons, for sure. They didn't want a 23-year-old-punkette telling them what to do. My mom was outraged. Especially with me! She gave me "Lecture Number 128" on how I needed to love myself more. My self-esteem was in the gutter. My mom challenged me to take a few moments each day to cultivate the simple practice of calling forth my inner loving.

So everyday for a week, I called forth my inner loving. With that, I noticed that I started to make more self-loving and self-nurturing choices. Then I began to call forth the loving in each of my Board members. On the night of the Board meeting, I walked in a little late and said, "You know, I'm sorry I'm late. Thank you for having me here tonight. Go ahead. You can proceed with the meeting." And I just sat there in full confidence and fulfillment. From that meeting on, they always made sure I was included.

If you are completely established in the consciousness of love, you project love to everyone all the time—not just when they are loving, but even when they are unloving. That whole experience taught me that there is nothing more important to your happiness and your well-being than enhancing the flow of self-love. The way you feel about yourself has a profound effect on every aspect of your life—from how you treat others, to the choices you make about your work, to your personal relationships. When you love and value yourself, you make choices based on the belief that you deserve the best in life. Which of course you do.

As students of Truth, it is important to realize that you live at the very heart and center of the Love of God. Before you reach to your outer relationships, know that you are always in Love, and that Love is always in you. Thomas Merton wrote, "If you have love, you will do all things well." When you vibrate from that place, you become loved and lovable.

You know how it is. When you glow with love, how do people treat you? When you are happy and fulfilled, heads turn and sparkling eyes meet yours with warmth and love in return. Best of all, you don't have to give up a part of yourself to be in the company of others.

Whenever we give up a part of ourselves in attempt to cling to love, it is not a holy relationship. I have done that, more than once, and I am not doing it any more. When we give up who we are, we are essentially saying that we need to be less than our True Self in order to receive our good from another person. Not so! You are more than good enough, for God's Love is right inside of you and all around you.

Let God love you. You are never deficient in God's Love. Many times when I am feeling insecure about something, I say, "Spirit, love me into my full Being," and I just let that Love from within me expand outward. You fulfill the potential of your being when you come from that true nature. When you are in the flow of your true nature, which is Love, you will ultimately be fulfilled in all that you do. And you will fall in love with life.

I leave you with Emmet Fox's most famous and profound poem on love: "There is no difficulty that enough love will not conquer, no disease that enough love will not heal; no door that enough love will not open; no gulf that enough love will not bridge; no wall that enough love will not throw down; no sin that enough love will not redeem. It makes no difference how deeply seated may be the trouble; how hopeless the outlook; how muddled the tangle; how great the mistake. A sufficient realization of love will dissolve it all. If only you could love enough you would be the happiest and most powerful being in the world."

30.

God Makes A Way Out of No Way

L ast week I took my dad out for an early Father's Day breakfast. As I looked at him, I marveled at all that he has been and done for me in my life.

I enjoy the thrill of adventure in my life, and my dad gave me exactly that. When I was about six or so, he had me jump off cliffs into big lakes. We would take exciting trips into the jungles of South America. Sometimes, he would create some danger right at home. Like on a Sunday afternoon, he would grill an exotic "something" that we didn't want to know the name of. My dad would pour lighter fluid all over the charcoal and yell, "When I light this, RUN!" Sure enough, he would light it and we would run for dear life. Then we'd promptly return and say, "Wow, dad, can you do that again?!" My dad provided a lot of fun and adventure. He has always been my hero.

The ultimate hero would undoubtedly be God. He always provides for each one of us. In Isaiah 65:24 it states, "Before they call I will answer, while they are yet speaking, I will hear." Have you ever noticed when you look back on your life, that there is a Higher Order to things? When you look back at some of your life's disappointments, you see that they weren't really disappointments at all, but rather "His-appointments," where something bigger and greater than yourself was leading you to a better situation.

There is a unique orderliness to this Universe, a Divine Intelligence that is at work at all times and in all places. This Intelligence, God, is fully present right here, right now, right where you are, at every point across the earth and throughout the Universe. It knows what is best for you. Everything that you need exists exactly where you are at every moment of your life. There is no place where Divine Intelligence is not fully accessible. I am always blown away by this understanding, and love being reminded of it.

Know that there is no problem that God cannot solve. No matter what the problem is, no matter how big or small, important or unimportant, you are entitled to a miracle, because you are a child of God. We are told in the book *A Course in Miracles* that we do not ask God for too much, but for too little. The ultimate hero, God, who wants to provide for us, says, "Ask and ye shall receive even more." [Matthew 6:24-34]

Do you not see that there is a careful design of a Higher Power? That God knows what is best for each and every one of us? If God has a careful design for the lilies of the field and the birds of the air, does He not have a careful design for you? He does! And it is greater than you can imagine. If you look through the most powerful telescope into infinity in either direction, you see perfect order. Perfect order exists throughout the Universe. People, events and things are meticulously placed in our lives. Each one is a part of the plan.

There is only one situation in which you would not find perfect order, and that is in a person's life who thinks they have everything handled. That they are doing this thing called life all by themselves. They have probably been living their lives from a place of chaos. Why? Because they have been putting themselves first. Indeed, in our normal human condition, we think "me first" as in, "It's all about me, me, me. Okay, enough about me. What do think about me?"

What if instead we lived a day of putting God first? Where in everything you did, you reminded yourself, "Oh I am here by Divine appointment. What kind of miracle could be waiting for me?" God has a plan. Trust Him and put Him first.

Some of you may be thinking, "There is not a plan for my life! I pray, but it looks like life is getting worse." I have seen so many people throughout the years where devastating things happened in their lives, when they experienced challenges and setbacks. But a setback is really a set-up! It's a stepping-stone to a greater plan. For every disappointment, there is a His-appointment.

That is the way it works. A door closes. You see it as devastating. You wonder if you have what it's going to take to make it through this dreadful experience. And you pray, pray, pray! Then you begin to see that your Father-God knows best, and you move into a greater understanding that there truly is a Divine plan and a Universal order to all things.

When I got divorced, I felt that all the doors were closing. I had no place to live. I didn't have a job. My family lived out of state. I didn't know where to go. Then I started to see that each person who came into my life was really a set-up. They were setting me up for the bigger picture, God's picture.

We can only see fragments of that picture, but know that there is a bigger picture at work in you and for your highest good. If you are experiencing a major challenge in your life, and feel like there is no plan for you, that all the doors around you are closing, think again! The doors are just beginning to open. Was it not Jesus who said, "Are not five sparrows sold for two pennies, and not one of them is forgotten before God? Why even the hairs of your head are numbered." [Luke 12:6-7]

Nothing is left out or forgotten. You certainly have not been left out or forgotten! Everything has significance. Everything has meaning. Nothing is random or separate from God. It is wonderful to see how the Universe brings about various ways to assist, to support, and to connect you to your highest good.

Alan Cohen, author of many best-selling books, tells the story in *The Dragon Doesn't Live Here Any More* of how he once saw a small rat helping himself to food in his pantry. Alan bought a "Have a Heart" live-trap and caught the little rodent. The rat did not like being in a cage, and scurried about furiously to find a way out. Alan took the rat out to a nearby field to release him. Alan tilted the cage and opened the door for the critter to slide out, but the rat did not jump out. Instead, the rat clung to the cage with all its might. The more Alan shook the cage, the more that rat hung on. Finally, Alan shook the cage fiercely, and the rat slid out to its beautiful new home.

When I first heard that story, I couldn't help but think that when the doors appear to be closing all around us, we feel trapped. We hold on to the old because we fear that there is nothing better in store for us. But each time your cage is shaken, it is always being shaken toward something better. Doors *are* opening. Challenges come into your life not to destroy you, but to empower you.

Your part in this is to know that there is a greater design for your life. Surrender to God's Higher Order. Trust. As Albert Einstein so eloquently put it, "There are two ways to live your life—as if nothing is a miracle or as if everything is a miracle." When you find yourself challenged, ask yourself, "What miracle is coming out of this?" You may not know when or where you are going to meet your good, but when you surrender to God's plan, know that you will.

Everything in the Universe is of concern to God. You are not insignificant to God. God always makes a way out of no way!

Where's MY manifestation?!

Have you ever been in a situation where you ask yourself, "Why does everybody else get all the perks? Where's MY manifestation?" Well, my answer to that is—get on the frequency of enjoyment and gratitude!

When your channels are open, the goodness of life can't help but rush in. But there's another part to the answer, what author Pam Grout calls "the pinball theory." Do your thoughts resemble the formation of migrating geese, all flying in the same direction? Or are they more like what happens with a pinball machine?

Here's the pinball theory in practice. Let's say you ask the Universe for a relationship. But then you start wondering if you're really worthy, and then there's that last jerk/jerkette who was really a downer, and well, what if this new person sees your cellulite or beer belly or— oh, forget about it! And with that, you just pinballed yourself right out of your good.

There is never unwillingness or reluctance by the Universe to provide our good. It is the Father's good pleasure to give you the Kingdom! First, we've got to get out of pinball mode, and get all those geese flying in the same direction. So take a moment, get all your thoughts in alignment with where you want to go, and you will be astounded by the miraculous undertakings in your favor!

31.

Fear Not

Sometimes, the overwhelming fears or worries in our minds can defeat the all-possibility that we are, the value, the incredibleness of who we are. Sometimes, we think that we have overcome all fear. Then, something occurs and without warning—to our dismay—we are once again fearful and apprehensive.

A physical condition may cause us to be afraid. We may be called upon to do something for which we do not feel qualified or prepared. We fear failure. Our financial security may be threatened. We fear that we will not have the wherewithal to see ourselves through. Sometimes our fear is for another person. We are alarmed over a loved one's state of health or their safety. We picture dire happenings.

Fear, however, has no power except the power we give it through our thoughts. Fear is rarely based on fact. Usually fear is attached to something that is in the future, something that hasn't even happened. Fear can paralyze you. But you are not being stopped by something on the outside, rather by something on the inside. Fear is usually when you are alone in your head "without adult supervision."

We're afraid this isn't the right relationship, or we're afraid that it is. We're afraid someone won't like us, or we're afraid they will. We're afraid of failure, or we're afraid of success. We're afraid our candidate will not be elected, or we're afraid he or she will. Man's worst enemy through the ages has not been famine, war, poverty, crime or death, but fear. Fear is not only the most destructive of all human emotions, but it does more to kill ambition, destroy health and dull the faculties of the mind than any other emotion.

Some years ago, in Vero Beach, Florida, whales were beaching themselves on the shore to die. Scientist, perplexed, asked themselves, "What is going on? Why would these healthy, normal whales beach themselves?" The scientists dragged the whales back into the sea to try to save them, but the whales would just turn around and come back onto to shore, wanting to die. The scientists, with the help of underwater cameras, discovered that thousands—perhaps millions—of tiny fish, which literally overwhelmed the whales, were chasing the whales. Instead of turning around and facing their small enemies, the whales rushed to accept death, rather than the fear held in their minds.

So it is with humans. Ninety percent of all our fears are not real. Fear, as defined by Webster, is a painful emotion caused by a sense of impending danger or doom. Not a fact, but an *emotion*, which makes us do crazy things and causes useless, unnecessary suffering.

Fear can come in many different forms. Think of the last 24 hours. What percentage of those hours did you spend in little fears?

Maybe you were waiting for the "other shoe" to drop. Or perhaps you avoided certain people, not feeling good enough to allow others to know the real you. Maybe you said "yes" when you really wanted to say "no." Perhaps you worried for no obvious reason, but simply out of habit. You may have put your needs last, hoping to protect yourself from getting hurt by displeasing another. Perhaps you feared saying, "I love you" lest you weren't loved in return. Or maybe you were afraid to speak up, should you rock the boat and upset someone.

I don't know of a single human being who has not experienced fear. However I do know people who have not allowed fear to dominate their lives. The people who see that wherever there is fear, there is also the possibility of courage. The people who see that to be brave is not to be without fear, but to act in spite of fear. You see, these people certainly know fear, but they have learned how to handle it, to overcome it. They have learned how to make a fearful occasion an occasion to prove the power of God, an occasion to let the power of God, the courage of God, flow through themselves in strength and might.

We have been brought up in a world that does not always put God first. Where God is absent, is where fear steps in. According to *A Course in Miracles*, "The presence of fear is a sure sign that you are trusting only in your own strength." Do you remember Peter's little swimming accident, as related in the

Bible? [Matt. 14:22-32] When Peter turned away, he fell into the water. When he kept his gaze on Jesus, he didn't fall.

If you want to vanquish fear, keep your gaze on God. When you are willing to give your fears over to a Power much greater than the fear, your fears lose their power. The Power that God is rises up to say, "Fear not, I am with you." Did you know that the words "Fear not" appear 365 times in the Bible? Essentially God is saying, "Fear not" for each and every day of the year. The courageous and spiritual life is a life of oneness with God. It is not a life without challenge! Those who practice the spiritual life do not profess to be without fear, but are unwilling to go through their challenges without God. Fear is the absence of trust in God.

As Jane Drotar says, "Fear is simply faith pointed in the wrong direction." There is nothing to fear, for we are never alone. God's presence is always with us. We have spiritual assistance to aid and support us at all times.

When you call upon spiritual assistance, you vanquish any fear. You begin to live authentically, as who you truly are. You say "no" when you mean "no." You are willing to be wrong, and you are willing to be right. You are grateful for the good in your life. You give yourself a break, knowing you are doing your best. You praise yourself for all of your efforts. You dance down the hallway—wearing your favorite shirt—for no reason at all. You sing in the car, even though you are tone deaf. You are willing to fall in love. You wake up happy just to be alive. You say a resounding "Yes!" to yourself. That's the fearless life.

Let go of the fear and trust that God knows exactly what He is doing. Here's an affirmation to support you in doing that:

God stands before me.

God stands behind me.

God stands beside me.

God goes before me.

And whenever you feel fear come upon you, remember these beautiful words from the Bible:

The Lord is my Light and my salvation; whom shall I fear? The Lord is the strength of my Life; of whom shall I be afraid? [Psalm 27:1]

And it shall come to pass that the Lord shall give thee rest from thy fear. [Isiah 14:3]

Yea, though I walk through the valley of the shadow of death I shall fear no evil: for thou art with me. [Psalm 23:4]

Fear not for I am with thee. Be not dismayed, for I am your God: I will strengthen thee, I will help thee, and I will uphold thee. [Isiah 41:10]

Let not your heart be troubled, neither let it be afraid. [John 14:27]

Fear not, for it is the Father's good pleasure to give you the kingdom. [Luke 12:32]

32.

Compare and Despair

I was told a story once about a man named Morris who walked out into a New York City street one day, and presto! He got a taxi that was just going by. The cabbie said to him, "Perfect timing. You're just like Dave." Morris said, "Who?" The cabbie replied, "The late Dave Erikson. Now there's a guy who got everything right. Like my coming along when you needed a cab. It would have happened like that to Dave." Morris said, "Well, we all have our moments. But not everybody is lucky all the time."

The cabbie replied, "Dave was. He was a terrific athlete—tennis, golf, you name it. He sang like an opera baritone and danced like a Broadway star." Morris said, "Wow! He really must have been something, huh?" The cabbie continued, "Yep! He had a memory like a steel trap. Could remember everybody's birthday. He knew all about wine, which fork to eat with. He could fix anything. Not like me. I change a fuse, and I black out the whole neighborhood," Morris exclaimed, "Oh! No wonder you remember him." The cabbie said, "Well, I never actually met Dave." "Then how do you know so much about him?" asked Morris. The cabbie replied, "Because I married his widow."

Ever get the feeling that you never quite measure up to a standard that someone else has set? It can be very frustrating. We look around and see people who have achieved such great things in their professional lives, in their family lives, in their spiritual lives that we're left feeling very inadequate. Or sometimes others make the comparison for us, which makes us feel even worse.

A different kind of comparison can actually make us feel good. I heard a comedian say, "Remember how good you felt when your neighbor's house got struck by lightning because he had a new satellite dish?" Be honest! Haven't you ever felt the slightest, tiny, twinge of joy when someone who had a bit more than you experienced some kind of downfall?

It's hard not to compare.

For example, imagine that you are at a wedding reception where you don't really know anyone and you have been seated with the boring people. No one is saying much. If they say anything at all, it is about the weather or the economy. Nothing real interesting. Or they are busy texting other people. Boring, boring, boring. Then you look over at the table next to you and they are having the time of their lives. To make matters worse, those people keep erupting with laughter. Wouldn't you think, "I wish I were at that other table. They are having a much better time!"

You see, human beings are by nature driven to compare. Whenever we have an experience, we tend to compare to other people's experiences or to an ideal image that we have made up in our minds. When you compare yourself to others, you can always find someone greater than you are, which can easily create a sense of inadequacy and incompetence. Or you can always find someone worse than you are, and that can create a sense of pride and arrogance.

Truth be told, you cannot be happy and envious at the same time. In fact, one of the greatest secrets of having happiness in your life is to learn how to eliminate envy. Romans 12:6-8 states "Let's just go ahead and be what we were made to be, without enviously or pridefully comparing ourselves with each other, or trying to be something we aren't." We were made to be glorious in the eyes of God, just as we are, children of God in whom God is well pleased.

In the fourth century A.D., Evagrius Ponticus, a monk who lived for many years in the Egyptian desert, had a brilliant mind. He devoted 14 years of his later life to studying classical theological texts, and from those evolved his own book, *The Eight Deadly Thoughts*. Two centuries later, his work caught the attention of Pope Gregory I, who revised the book and published them under the title *The Seven Deadly Sins*.

Now, what is interesting is that the original *Eight Deadly Thoughts* stresses that you and I do not wrestle with sins so much as with erroneous thoughts. This makes sense because we all have thoughts that stir up emotional turmoil, yet we are not evil or sinful people just because we find ourselves thinking these "deadly thoughts." What we need to do is gain mastery over these thoughts. What are these thoughts? They are thoughts that lead to negativity or despair, gluttony, greed, sloth, sorrow, lust, anger, vanity and pride. Evagrius Ponticus warns us that the "comparison game" is what will lead to most of those deadly thoughts.

Whenever you compare your achievements with those of others, those deadly thoughts emerge, and you will be deeply disappointed. Rather than find joy in the glory of who we are right now, we think of all the pleasures we could have enjoyed were it not for our so-called failings.

Instead of comparing yourself to everybody else, take an elevated action. Learn! Learn from everybody. For example, I learn from Churches that are bigger than ours and Churches that are smaller than ours. I learn from critics. I learn from people I may not agree with. I learn from everybody who can offer a more expanded, elevated way of going about life.

If you are humble and approach life with a "beginner's mind," the Zen mind, you can learn from anybody. When you refuse to learn from others, it's because you're allowing your ego to get in the way of your living a more expanded life. Your pride is ruling you.

This understanding is nothing new. Since before Buddha, spiritual masters have been saying the same thing over and over again. Jesus didn't say anything new. Our co-founders Charles and Myrtle Fillmore didn't say anything new. New Thought leaders and authors of today like Deepak Chopra, Wayne Dyer, Marianne Williamson and Louise Hay—none of them are saying anything new. I'm not even saying anything new!

When you come with a beginner's mind to the various experiences and people in your life, you awaken to your Highest Self, your innermost highest vibration. That's why we come to Church every Sunday! To come back home to our inner highest vibration, the Christ within. If you refuse the beginner's mind, if you close your mind to what you might learn, if you stay stuck in comparison, you will go into despair.

A colleague once told me that comparing herself to others caused financial problems because she would then buy things she didn't need, with money she didn't have, to impress people she didn't like. Comparing herself to others caused marital problems because the grass could start looking greener on the other side of the fence. Comparing herself to others caused spiritual problems because she was not present to her own divinity and her own unique talents.

Comparison is hell! I know this all too well. A few years ago, our Church rent went up significantly and we weren't able to afford it. We had to be fiscally responsible and move from the building we occupied, which was a space I really liked. I felt like a failure at the time. Plus, there were people around me who had strong opinions that drove the feeling of failure even deeper into me. I began comparing myself as a Minister to other Ministers and our Church to other Churches. I was coveting and feeling less than.

Now I am going to press the pause button on my "woe-is-me" victim story for a moment to share a lesson in the anatomy of how comparison operates.

When you compare, an internal voice criticizes you and lashes out at you. You feel like you are under attack. Because your brain does not distinguish between imagination and reality, these internal attacks are perceived by the mind as real. Scientists have found that when self-criticism takes place, the human body shoots adrenaline and cortisol (the stress hormone) through its veins. Your heart rate gets erratic, and your breathing becomes rapid. Your body's ability to repair muscle, your digestion, as well as your cognitive reasoning, are all impaired. We aren't even aware that all this is going on inside of us, for the body reacts unconsciously.

That inner self-critic is one of the most common obstacles that gets in the way of your brilliance. Physically, your body feels like it is under attack. Emotionally, we experience a sense of shame. Dr. Brene Brown, author of *The Gifts of Imperfection*, states, "Shame is the intensely painful feeling or experience of believing that we are flawed, and therefore unworthy of love and belonging." We feel isolated, we are assailed by feelings of self-doubt, we lack confidence in our ability to achieve things. We feel like we are just not good enough—for pretty much anything. And we usually think that we're the only one on the planet who's suffering from these negative thoughts and feelings.

One of the main reasons we are so affected by our negative thoughts is that we think our mind has an accurate grasp on reality. Yet that is often not the case. Our mind's view may be very distorted. A friend of mine reminded me, during my time of shame and woe over our Church move, "You know you are not alone in this experience. With about seven billion people on the planet, I can guarantee that you are not the only one going through the exact same thing at this very moment." That truly was an "aha!" moment for me. Her words helped me think, not only of others who have experienced what I was going through, but also of those who were a few steps ahead of me. That triggered me to *learn* rather than compare.

Instead of saying, "Why don't I have that?" from my place of victim consciousness, I started asking, "How can I have that?

What do I need to learn to get that?" Which then transformed into, "I can have that!" Do you see the difference? Comparing is indulging in victim consciousness, whereas learning is empowering! I then sought out others who had what I wanted, and asked for their help and assistance. I was able to learn from them the valuable lessons I needed for the next even-better phase of my—and my Church's—life.

Instead of playing "small" by comparing yourself to others, feeling shame and feeling inadequate, play "big." Be willing to learn, so your experience can shift you into better and happier ways of being, into an ever more joyous and successful life.

33.

Wired for Divine Guidance

A woman decided to go horseback riding on day. The horse started off at a slow gallop. The woman was thoroughly enjoying the ride, but then the horse launched into a canter and she lost control. The woman slide off the saddle, but her right foot was still in the stirrup. As the horse kept going so did she! The woman could not get her foot out of the stirrup. In a panic she yelled for help. It was soon after she started screaming at the top of her lungs that the mall customer satisfaction representative went over to the mechanical horse and pulled the plug.

That story reminded me of a bumper sticker, "Ever stop to think, and then forget to start again?" There certainly are times when we aren't very intelligent. Such as when we make a choice that is not for our highest good even while a voice inside us is screaming "no."

We are all wired to know the intelligence of God—it is working through us all the time. The intelligence of God is what allows us to know things that we have no way of knowing—but somehow we do. The key is to listen to that knowing and act on it. Yet many times, we act against it because we are also wired to choose whether we are going to use Divine Intelligence.

We have been given the gift of choice, and with that, we can choose human intelligence or Divine Intelligence. Every year we are given approximately 525,600 minutes—525,600 gifts. We can choose those minutes in confusion, resentment, guilt or anger if we so desire. Or we can choose to use our gift of time toward that which is worthwhile, helpful, healthy, healing, positive, peace making and for the highest good of all concerned.

The routines of everyday life, such as going to work or to school, our daily chores and family obligations, don't make big demands on our ability to make good choices. But when important choices and decisions must be made about career direction, change of residence or a pending marriage or partnership, many times we feel ill equipped to make the right choice. It is when we are having to make tough and difficult decisions that we must rely on Divine Intelligence, on God's wisdom, not our own. Sometimes we forget that at all times, in all situations, we are connected to the awesome, powerful intelligence of God. That is how we are wired. To be a channel of His intelligence, if we let Him.

God's intelligence is always good, ever guiding us into right and perfect ways. So why do we insist upon doing it our way? Why don't we let the intelligence of God work through our lives?

Because we don't trust His intelligence. It is all a matter of what we trust. If we are trusting a problem, we lose sight that we are forever one with the intelligence of God. We are not, we cannot be, separated from Divine Intelligence. If we persist in feeling separated by choosing to be worried, angry or resentful, it is no wonder that we find ourselves confused, depressed and overwhelmed.

Although it is human nature to try to figure things out and to do things our way, we must learn to trust the intelligence of God. When you listen to Divine Intelligence, you know without a doubt that what may seem impossible to you is possible to God. Nothing is undeserving of God's help, no matter how large or how small. When you listen to Divine Intelligence you cannot lose.

Those of you who have been divorced know what a hard decision it can be. I remember wrestling with the decision to divorce my then husband. It was one of the most excruciating decisions I have ever had to make. I questioned myself. I tried to sort out pros and cons. We went to counseling. I sought support from fellow Ministers. I felt myself collapsing into fears that virtually paralyzed me.

In the midst of that turmoil I got down on my knees and asked for Divine Intelligence to help me make a choice. I was then filled with a peace beyond all understanding, and I had the overwhelming feeling that I wasn't alone, that God was my partner in this. With that, my then husband and I made a mutual decision to go our separate ways. We ended up better friends than we ever were spouses. I consider him a dear part of my life.

When life seems to burden us with more than we can—or even want to— handle, it is not that we cannot handle it. It is that we do not know *how* to handle it. As humans, we try even harder, we exude even more energy, we become even more determined And yet, all we need to do is relax and listen to the intelligence of God within.

I can't tell you how many people have come into my office after they have broken up with someone, saying, "I knew not to get involved with this person, but did I listen? No! I saw and heard the red flags, but did I act on them? No!" We need to listen and rely on God's wisdom to show us the way. In Joshua 24:15 it states, "Choose you this day whom you will serve. As for me and my house, we will serve the Lord." Our choices determine our lives.

Who will you serve this day? Your Divine Intelligence or your human will? You always have a choice. For example, you can choose to release "artificial littleness," meaning that when you choose a limiting thought, you can say "no" to that thought. You can say "no" to believing that you are little or not worthwhile, "no" to self-pity, "no" to victimhood, "no" to defeatism or pessimism. When you say "no" to littleness, you can hear the Presence. You can hear Divine Intelligence, which is not an invitation to slip into "inauthentic bigness," or "puffed-up-ness," as in "Look what I'm doing!" Remember, "It is not I, but the Father within who is doing His works." [John 14:10]

Release artificial littleness, surrender inauthentic bigness and honor the greatness of God and all His intelligence; you will become a channel through which greatness is given form. You will then tap into a grace that will astound you. You will begin to attract people, situations and circumstances that are greater than anything you can imagine. After all, that is how you are wired—to listen, honor and give form to God's intelligence.

Here is an exercise to help you use your power of Divine intelligence effectively. Sit quietly and breathe deeply as you repeat the statement, "I am now open and receptive to the intelligence of God." Practice feeling the presence of God. Then ask a question concerning your specific situation. "Should I take this job?" "Is moving out of state for my highest good?" If you experience a sense of expansion, then your answer is to move forward. If you experience a feeling of contraction, then you will know what not to do. If you have difficulty experiencing either feeling, repeat to yourself, "God loves me and God cares for me, and the intelligence of God is upon me." Eventually you will sense God's presence guiding you to your highest good.

God's intelligence is upon you now and always, blessing you, encouraging you, helping you, uplifting you, sustaining you, protecting you, guiding you and directing you. Allow His intelligence to move through you, and your life will be blessed indeed!

34.

A Clean Sweep

One winter, our Church office in Denver was without heat for over two weeks. The office was located in a little carriage house which had, of all things, a chimney. The pipe that releases carbon monoxide from the boiler through the chimney was blocked and toxic carbon monoxide was backing up into the house. Of course the boiler had to be turned off, and thus, no heat. When we investigated the situation, we discovered debris at the bottom of the chimney—dead squirrels and ivy—blocking the proper release of carbon monoxide. Getting a chimney sweep at that time of year was virtually impossible.

However, I found the whole experience to be an excellent metaphor for how we sometimes operate in life.

There are times when our spiritual channels are not open and because of that, we become toxic. At which point we wonder why the world responds to us the way it does. I call it spiritual cellulite—a morass of accumulated sludge and fatty deposits of unforgiveness, holding grudges or blaming others. When the chimney was blocked in our little carriage house, I had to take a look at my own spiritual channel. Was I blaming anyone? Was I not forgiving someone? Of course, my first thought was, "Oh, not me! I'm so pure!"

But guess what? I found a couple of "dead squirrels" way down in the bottom of my spiritual chimney/channel. In particular, I was surprised to find that there were some people I had not forgiven. It was not easy for me to forgive them, yet I knew I must. You see, when you withhold forgiveness or love from anyone, it diminishes your awareness of the abundance of good in your life. You are stuck in so much old stuff that the new good stuff has no way of getting to you. In essence, the good that you withhold from others will be withheld from you.

I challenge you to be honest and ask yourself whether or not your spiritual chimney is clean. You too, may be surprised. If you want more good to come into your life, take the time to look and see who you haven't forgiven.

Charles Fillmore reminds us in his book, *Prosperity*, of the Lord's Prayer [Matthew 6:12] "Forgive us our debts, as we also have forgiven our debtors." Fillmore writes that, "In these words Jesus expressed an infallible law of mind, the law that one idea must be dissolved before another can take its place. If you have in your mind any thought that someone has wronged you, you cannot let in the cleansing power of Spirit and the richness of spiritual substance until you have cast out the thought of the wrong, have forgiven it fully. You may be wondering why you have failed to get spiritual illumination or to find the consciousness of spiritual substance. Perhaps the reason is here: a lack of room for the true thoughts because other thoughts fill your mind. If you are not receiving the spiritual understanding you feel you should have, you should search your mind carefully for unforgiving thoughts. "Thoughts are things" and occupy space in the mind realm. They have substance and form and may easily be taken as permanent by one not endowed with spiritual discernment. They bring forth fruit according to the seed planted in the mind."

It is forgiveness that will clean out your spiritual chimney. Forgiveness invokes the spirit of grace, which will then wash over you and purify your entire being. It is a clean sweep - and how sweet it is. Forgiveness, however, is one of the least understood of all spiritual practices. Most people believe that when you forgive someone, you are doing something for *them*. The truth is, when you forgive, you are doing it for *yourself*. In forgiving, whether it be forgiving others or ourselves, we make the journey from guilt or anger to a clean slate and a new beginning.

That transformation comes about as we reflect on the results of our mistakes, understanding how our ignorance or our emotional wounds prompted our actions or reactions. Because, like it or not, you were born human. And being human means that we are capable of making mistakes. There is not a person alive who has not made a mistake. Indeed, to err is human, to forgive is divine. However, one of the worst mistakes we can make is when we think that our mistakes, or the ones that others attribute to us, are indications of who we are or what we deserve. Do not define yourself by your mistakes!

Once upon a time, there was a man who stole a piece of bread. He was caught and was immediately taken to his King.

The King said, "This man shall be hanged." As was the custom, before he was taken to be hanged, the man was asked if he had any last words. The thief said, "King, know this. Know that I can take an apple seed. I can plant that apple seed and it will grow and bear fruit overnight. It is a secret that my father taught me. I do not think that this secret should die with me." Well, the King was mightily intrigued. It was decided that the next day the thief, the King and all of the King's men would learn the secret of planting seeds that bear fruit overnight.

The thief dug a hole and then stood back with the seed in his hand. He said, "Anyone who has stolen, anyone who has taken anything from anyone, cannot plant this seed. I am a thief, therefore I am unable to plant this seed." The King called forth his Prime Minister to plant the seed. The Prime Minister hesitated, and said, "Oh King. I am sorry to say that a number of years ago I took something that did not belong to me, and I didn't say anything to anyone, so I cannot plant that seed." Whereupon the King summoned his Treasurer, who said, "King, I cheated some people out of their money. This was a long time ago, but I did cheat some people out of their money, so I cannot plant that seed." Then the King reflected. He thought about the time when he took something very precious from his father. So the King himself could not plant the seed.

The thief turned to the King and all his men, and said, "You are all powerful and mighty. You are not in want of anything. Yet not one of you can plant this seed. I, who stole a little food to stay alive, am to be hanged." The King was impressed with the thief's wisdom. He pardoned him and asked the thief for forgiveness. All went their separate ways, better off by far for the experience.

Doesn't this story sound familiar? John 8:7, "But when they persisted in asking him, he straightened up and said to them, "He who is without sin among you, let him be the first to throw a stone at her." One of the greatest lessons that Jesus wanted us to learn and remember was the lesson of forgiveness. Forgive yourself, he said, forgive your neighbor. Not just seven times, but seventy times seven!

When we are confronted with hurtful events it is wise to remember Joseph's experience as described in the Old Testament. People in Joseph's life treated him horribly, but he kept saying, "You meant this for evil, but God meant it for good." Indeed, fabulous events came out of those horrendous experiences. Usually we say, "You meant it for evil, it feels like evil, and there is nothing good about it." But when you can find the good, it is simple to forgive.

How do you find the good? To see it, to know it, to feel it, first you must look for it. You must train your eye only on what is good. If you habitually look for bad, bad is all you will see and you will stay victim to the unhappy circumstance.

Now some of you might be asking questions such as:

What is good about betrayal?

What is good about lying and cheating?

What is good about abuse—mental, emotional or physical?

What is good about divorce?

What is good about war, poverty, or murder?

What is good about homelessness, cancer or aids?

There is much good that comes out of these things! Consider Anne Frank, Helen Keller, Christopher Reeves. Despite outwardly inhuman challenges and conditions, they all found their good embedded in, because of, and in spite of, their challenges and conditions. How? These remarkable people looked inward. They changed their thinking and with that, their realizations guided them to become beacons of love and enlightenment. They consciously chose to find their good. They decided that good existed in their lives and in the lives of others.

Each of them could have elected to remain locked within their bodies and their situations, blaming God, bad genes, or bad luck. If they had, the world would be the poorer for it. But luckily for us, they found their good. They forgave their situations and found their mission. And then what did these amazing individuals do? They gave it away. They shared their good with us.

It is through challenge that you grow and evolve. You discover strengths that you would not ordinarily know existed within yourself, within the people you love, even within complete strangers. You learn compassion for your fellow humans. You learn to appreciate the good that is already in your life. You learn what is of value to you, what you desire to spend your time on during the precious moments of your life. Therein lies the glory of being human. Therein lies the good.

Forgiving is a way to focus your eye on the good in yourself and the good in others. To forgive is to release what is false for what is true. It is a way to end the search for love out there. It is a way to give love from within yourself. Through the process of forgiveness you learn to love yourself and you learn to love others.

As has been said many times, "You are a spiritual being having a human experience." Be the spiritual being you truly are. Look in your chimney—your spiritual channel—and see if there are any dead squirrels clogging up the free flow of your good.

Forgive, release, let go and let God!

Scary Hostage-Takers

Have you ever felt that you were held hostage in a conversation? Maybe to a family member, a friend, a co-worker or boss who chattered endlessly and you couldn't seem to get away? Well, we can say the same for our emotions. There are emotions that keep us hostage on a daily basis: fear, regret, anger and resentment. They keep us captive to a smaller life, a life of less. Fear, regret, anger and resentment are not only hostage-takers, they're energy vampires, deluding us into thinking an unhappy life is the one and only version of life we will ever have. But these hostage-takers are only imagined.

You are free to escape from your fears, regrets, anger and resentments at any time. Realize that it is you who are feeding these hostage-takers. It is you who are keeping them alive and safe. Not only that, you've come to believe that these hostage-takers are the ones who are making the demands. The truth is, you are the one who is in charge of any demands. And it is time for you to demand your freedom. Time for you to demand a larger, more abundant life! Time to recognize your scary hostage-takers for who they are: soul-suckers, freedom-thieves, love-stealers, peace-abductors and joy-leakers!

It is time to finally escape from your fears, regrets, anger and resentments, to choose a lighter, happier way of thinking! For then a larger, more expanded, joyful life awaits you.

35.

Perfectly Imperfect

A notice on the bulletin board at our local grocery store caught my eye:

LOST

Dog with 3 legs, blind in his left eye.

Missing right ear, tail broken.

Recently castrated.

Answers to the name of "Lucky."

I ask you, is anything really perfect?

As human beings, we are not perfect and that is perfectly all right. However, many people spend their entire lives trying to be perfect. But no one is perfect in this physical world, and no one ever was or shall be. Not only that, but there is no way to please a perfectionist.

I have never met a perfectionist whose life was filled with inner peace. The need for perfection and the desire for inner tranquility are at odds. When we are attached to having something be a precise way, we are bound to run into frustration. When we focus on what's wrong, when we fail to be content with what is, we cannot help but be dissatisfied and discontent. The very act of focusing on imperfection pulls us away from our purpose of being kind, understanding, compassionate and gentle with one another.

This is not to imply that you should cease to do your very best or to take care of yourself if something in your life is uncomfortable or downright bad. Nor does it mean that you cannot improve yourself or that you should just resign yourself to your lot in life. Rather it is the willingness to take a look at where we are overly focused on what's wrong in life. It's about realizing that while there's always a better way to do things, it doesn't mean that we can't enjoy and appreciate the way things are. There is perfection within the imperfection.

In the movie "Brother Sun, Sister Moon," Pope Innocent tells St. Francis, "In our obsession with original sin, we have forgotten Original Innocence."

The key to peace of mind is to realize that everything is perfectly imperfect. I remember shopping with my mom when we were on vacation in Mexico. She bought a dozen or so blue cobalt drinking glasses that were all different shapes and sizes. I said, "Mom, you are buying a bunch of glasses that don't match." She said, "I know. They are perfectly imperfect, just like we are."

We live in a world that is not perfect, full of people who have their quirks and situations that are messy. We may even have what we consider to be the perfect mate, the perfect car, or the perfect house, but somewhere down the road imperfections will appear, because everything changes. If nothing else, all things eventually need maintenance and that is perfectly alright.

I've had countless women and men come into my office saying, "I've just met the nicest man or woman, but she's somewhat over weight, or he's losing his hair, or she's a bit chatty, or he's not very tall," and the list goes on. I remind them that we are all guaranteed to get a little saggy and wrinkly and possibly lose our hair. It is what's inside that counts.

Some things in life are not how you would have them be. You have to adjust. Being willing to adjust to the imperfections is a sign of acceptance.

A mother was disappointed with her child. They were at odds with each other all the time, until the mother came across an anonymous paragraph that completely changed their relationship:

Acceptance is the answer to all my problems today. When I am disturbed, it is because I find some person, place, thing or situation, some fact in my life, unacceptable to me and I can find no serenity until I accept that that person, thing, or situation as being exactly the way it is supposed to be at this moment. Unless I accept life completely on life's terms, I cannot be happy. I need to concentrate not so much on

what needs to be changed in the world as what needs to
be changed in me and my attitude.

One of life's paradoxes is that in order to change an unwanted situation, we must first accept it the way it is. If you wish to move forward in your life, first make peace with what you are presently experiencing. As Jesus said, "Agree with thine adversary quickly" [Matthew 5:25]. Acceptance is that moment when you admit the truth of where you are. You do not have to like what is going on in your life, but you must accept it, whatever it is. As long as you do not accept reality, you are powerless to define the role you will play.

Failure to accept reality is a denial of your power to make a conscious choice. When you do not choose, you live by default. You are a victim to circumstances. You have forgotten that all of our imperfect experiences, no matter how awful they may appear, are temporary. Accepting does not mean you approve. Acceptance simply means that that you are able to withdraw your emotional attachment just long enough to see what is actually happening.

Without the emotional charge, you may even discover that what is happening has nothing to do with you. You see it, feel it and may even know that something must be done. However, it is only from the emotionally detached place of acceptance that you can make a wise choice. You must release the fantasy in your mind to enter the real world of truth and facts.

Acceptance is an act of courage. Acceptance requires that you allow something you were not willing to see before to be revealed to you.

A friend showed up one day on my door step. She was

continually verbally abused by her kids. Anytime I went over to her house, I was appalled at how her children treated her. I asked her once, "Are you going to let them treat you like that?" She couldn't answer. She was so used to the abuse. So when she showed up at my door, she had finally accepted reality. She saw her situation for what it was, abusive. By accepting what was, she was keenly aware of what wasn't. From there she was able to determine what she must do.

How many of us have been in similar situations in our relationships, our careers or our finances? When you accept the reality of your life, you demonstrate your willingness to make a conscious choice. You honor the wisdom, strength and persistence of God. God who *is* perfect, can master any adverse circumstance that appears in your life.

Acceptance is a type of surrender to something that is bigger than ourselves, to a Universe that knows what it is doing. When we surrender to God, we let go of our attachment to how things "should" happen and allow the Universe to do a much better job than we could.

Have the courage to see that what is, is. Let go of the emotional charge of anger, fear or victimization, know that all is imperfectly perfect, and with God, move on to greater good.

36.

The Mental Negativity Diet

Slander is defined as making a false statement that damages a person's reputation. We don't think of gossip in that way, but gossip is a form of slander. It's most often putting someone down, talking badly against them.

Over the years, people have come to me when friends have turned against them, or they'd been cheated or lied about. They were struggling against a mighty temptation to defend themselves and attack back. But *A Course in Miracles* states, "In our defenselessness, our safety lies." Meaning that if you just step back and let God lead the way, your good will come to you. And Jesus said [Matthew 5:38-40 NIV]: "You have heard that it was said, 'Eye for eye, and tooth for tooth.' But I tell you, do not resist an evil person. if anyone slaps you on the right cheek, turn to them the other cheek also. And if anyone wants to sue you and take your shirt, hand over your coat as well."

One of my favorite medieval stories begins with a man in a confession booth. The man says, "Father I have sinned. I have spread a falsehood about someone. I need forgiveness." The priest responds in traditional fashion, "On the basis of Christ's atoning work on your behalf and your repentance of sin, you are forgiven. As your first penance, you are to take a down pillow, cut it open and walk through the city, spreading the feathers everywhere. Then return to me, and I will reveal your next penance."

The man faithfully follows the priest's instructions. He goes through the city, spreading the feathers. He returns to the Church and asks the priest what he is to do next. "Now go," the priest responds, "and collect every one of those feathers." The man exclaims, "That would be impossible!" To which the priest replies, "You are right, and you are forgiven. But it is impossible to ever undo all the harm you've done with your gossip. Go and sin no more."

Whether you are reading a tabloid in the checkout line at the supermarket, hanging around the lunchroom to get the latest on your office mates or Facebooking to get the scoop on someone, there is just something intriguing about what others are doing. We've all done it! As Will Rogers said, "The only time people dislike gossip is when you gossip about them."

There are people who love to be up on the latest gossip, and are bursting at the seams to share it with you. Often we do listen to it and forget Jesus' stern words to the man whose speech whose speech impediment he cured. [Mark 7:36] "Tell no one! Do not gossip about this miracle." Jesus did all he could to keep his works a secret, off the Galilee grapevine. He knew that the tongue may well be the sharpest knife in the drawer. His mother, Mary, also knew the value of not spreading information. When her world was rocked by the news that she was with child, [Luke 2:19] "Mary kept all these things, and pondered them in her heart."

You must never be too busy, too tired or too pressured to check the accuracy of the data that comes your way. It is critical to greet any gossip you hear with a healthy skepticism. For if you don't, like Mary, "keep and ponder," before talking and proclaiming, you can inflict heavy pain and damage to people, their careers, companies, communities or even yourself.

The power of rumors, of bad information, to wreak havoc is even recognized by the New York Stock Exchange. Its Rule 435 states that it is illegal to spread rumors on the floor of the stock exchange, even when no overt fraud is intended. I think Rule 435 should be installed everywhere. I was once asked to help repair a Church where a group of people had spread rumors about others in the Church. The rumors so destroyed community morale and the group's harmony that the Church was foundering. I tried everything I could to get that Church back into working order, but to no avail. The Church never was able to get back on its feet. Nothing rips apart the foundation of any organization more dangerously or drastically than bad information and rumor mongering.

I remember being about seven years old, when I overheard my parents say that the parents of one of my friends, Connie*, were getting a divorce. So of course I couldn't wait to get to school and tell my other girlfriend, Judy. As I told Judy about Connie's parents, I didn't realize that Connie was right behind me. She did not know that her parents were about to get a divorce. Connie cried. She told her brother, who also cried, and then the two went home to tell their parents what I had said. Connie's parents naturally called my parents—which ultimately ruined their friendship. I learned at a very young age that gossip can destroy relationships and split people apart.

Maybe one of the reasons why people like to gossip is that they want to please and be accepted. If that is the case, who are you trying to please? By whom do you want to be accepted? Jesus said [John 5:30 ERV], "I can do nothing alone. I judge only the way I am told. And my judgment is right, because I am not trying to please myself. I want only to please the One who sent me." Jesus knew exactly who he wanted to please.

Who do you want to please the most? If it's God, then you can survive whatever is thrown at you. If it's people, then you are likely to be often disappointed and hurt, because you simply cannot please all of the people all of the time. Or even some of the people most of the time!

Be a God pleaser, not a people pleaser. You'll enjoy positive interactions with the people in your life, healthier relationships and—best of all—a happier you! It takes effort to break a lifetime habit of gossiping, but the results are worth it. When people clean up their speech, they clean up their lives. Suddenly, self-respect is enhanced and the respect of others is earned. You look at the world in a completely different way, and the world looks at you in a whole new light.

Years ago, I came across *The Seven Day Mental Diet* by Emmet Fox—a concept that literally changed my life. At the time, as I was going through a rough patch, I complained and indulged in gossip because it made me feel better to talk about someone else's problems than my own. When I read *The Seven*

Day Mental Diet, I realized that thought and speech are the real causative force in life. In other words, you cannot change your environment while leaving your mind and speech unchanged.

This, then, is the real key to a better life. When you change your thought and your speech, your body must change for the better, your daily activities must change for the better, your home must change for the better and your relationships must change for the better.

Emmet Fox challenges us to go on a "mental negativity diet" for seven days—to resist dwelling for a single moment on any kind of negative thought or speech. He is not saying that such thoughts won't come, just that we are not to *dwell* on those thoughts. He gives the example of a man who is sitting by an open fire when a red-hot cinder flies out and falls on his sleeve. If the man knocks that cinder off at once, no harm is done. But if the man allows the cinder to rest on his sleeve for even a single moment, it will burn a sizeable hole in his sleeve.

So it is with negative thought and speech. Watch yourself for a whole week and do not, under any circumstance, allow your mind or your speech to dwell on anything that is not positive, constructive, optimistic or kind. If you mess up, you need to start again. When I took on the mental diet challenge, I needed to start over again several times before I could get through the entire seven days! If you choose to accept the challenge, it is safe to say that your whole life will change for the better.

Here are some tips on how to navigate the negative thoughts or speech you may encounter as you go about your mental diet.

1. *Keep walking*

If you are at a social gathering, and you find yourself in a group of people talking negatively about someone, keep walking until you find a group of people speaking more positively.

2. *Educate those involved*

Let people know that you are on a diet from negativity, and ask for their support in keeping any conversation positive.

3. *Change the subject*

If someone continues to talk negatively, and you have to work or be in them vicinity, change the subject. Jump in with an exciting announcement regarding your football team, the weather, a cute story about one of your kids or dogs. Anything to distract the speaker long enough that the flow of conversation is redirected into something positive.

4. *Zone out*

Think about a hundred things other than what the speaker is saying—your grocery list, that funny thing you heard on a podcast, how blue the sky is, etc.

5. *See the Christ in others*

When you find yourself wanting to think negatively about someone, deliberately see the Christ in them. This will change your thought quickly.

The whole idea is to have seven days of unbroken mental discipline. Remember, nothing said or done by anyone else can possibly throw you off the diet, only your reaction to what they say or do. As you keep your thoughts and speech free of negativity, of gossip or slander, your life will change. You will be able to see the good in all things. You will see only solutions, not problems. You will come from a place of self-respect and self-love, and you will find yourself saying repeatedly, "What a great life I am living!"

Now, you will see through the eyes of God, and you will remember Jesus' words [Hebrews 10:9], "Lo, I come to do Thy will, O God." And His will is very, very good indeed!

* Names changed to protect privacy.

37.

You Can't...But God Can

"When we speak to God we are said to be praying, but when God speaks to us we are said to be schizophrenic."

—Lily Tomlin

A clever, funny quote, no doubt. But it hides a profound Truth—that there is a difference between being delusional and being spiritual.

We are delusional when we listen to what Buddhists call the "monkey mind," the voices that judge and criticize ourselves or others negatively. The voices that guide us away from Divine Assistance, voices that create fear and separation. They are the voices that tell you that *you* are in control, not God. Yet often, we give our power and attention to these voices, especially when we have a problem in our lives.

However, you can come to God even with all those other voices pestering you and ask for help. *A Course in Miracles* states,

"You do not have to purify your thoughts before coming to me. I am the purifier." But then the Course continues with, "I can't take away from you anything that you won't release."

The moment you align with God, the moment you ask for His help, the moment you surrender, is the moment that you realize Divine Assistance is available right here and right now. When you just let go of all your frustrations, concerns and worries, Divine Assistance comes rushing forth. When you allow Divine Assistance in, you see that there is another way. When you hear the voice of God, you know that what you are doing is the right thing. You have perceptual clarity.

When human beings were about to be created, an ancient Hindu myth has it that a committee of Gods got together to decide where the secret of life should be placed. The secret of life contained all of the Divine Assistance one could possibly imagine. All the Gods agreed that the secret should be hidden somewhere clever, but the Gods had a hard time agreeing where it should be hidden so as to make it most challenging for people to locate the treasure.

"Let us hide the secret of life at the top of the highest mountain!" one God suggested. "No! No!" replied another. "People will invent airplanes and helicopters and climbing equipment. Then everyone will be able to get to it." "How about at the bottom of the sea?" another God asked. "Same thing. They will invent submarines and diving equipment, and that will be the end of the game," replied another God. The Gods sat around for days, stumped as to where to hide the secret of life. "I have it!" exclaimed one of the Gods. "Let's hide the answer within each person. They'll never think to look there!"

And so it turned out that when we look for Divine Guidance, we tend to look outside ourselves for the answers. We listen to all those other voices. The last place we look is to the God within. Meanwhile, all that we ever need to know abides right there, at the core of our being. When we let go and allow God to have His say, Spirit has a chance to deliver its message when you need it the most.

Guidance often arrives in uncanny and synchronistic ways. One evening many years ago, I lived in the mountains of Boulder, Colorado. As I drove home from a class, terribly depressed, I was talking to God, asking Him for specific guidance. You see, I was contemplating asking my then husband for a divorce. We had tried everything—counseling, classes, healers and prayer. Yet nothing seemed to be making things better between us.

As I was driving home, I asked God to give me a sign, and asked that this sign give me the strength for whatever it was I needed to do. Just then, a mountain lion ran out in front of my car and stopped! We stared at each other for at least a minute before the lion turned and walked away. It was as if this lion was giving me her strength and power. In that moment, I aligned with God. I surrendered to something a lot bigger than my problem.

It was a tremendous moment that literally transformed my life. I was changed inside, and I knew that I would never be the same. That night as I walked in the door, hardly any words needed to be exchanged, for both of us knew what we needed to do to get on with our lives.

There comes a time in the life of every individual to experience this type of great moment. It is when the ego or all of those monkey mind voices come under the influence of a power much greater than themselves. It can happen in the twinkling of an eye.

When we align with God, God does not demand that you do not have negative voices within you. God simply demands that you have none that you would entertain and keep. It is unholy to keep thoughts that keep us separated from the good of God. When we entertain those other voices, those negative thoughts, we are in essence saying that we trust them more than we trust God. We have forgotten who walks beside us and who lives within us.

Beware! Because as soon as you forget God, insanity takes its course, and it feels like all hell is breaking loose.

Guess what those other voices feed off of? Control—our desire to control other people, situations, circumstances and places. When we try to be in control, life feels insane. God can work for you only as He can work through you. He can't very well work through you when you are listening to those voices that tell you to judge, be fearful, be critical and to be in control.

As I once heard Patrice Karst, author of *The Invisible String*, say, "The fact is that He who created butterfly wings and the Grand Canyon knows what He is doing, so you may want Him to lead for a change."

I would like to share with you something I use quite a bit. It is one of the ways I let go of control. It's called the "God Can." You can make your own "God Can" out of an empty tea canister, a glass jar or any other container as long as you label it as your "God Can." Now, the "God Can" is a powerful tool, especially for the subconscious mind, because the subconscious mind needs to see physical evidence of letting something go.

For instance, a mother I know was always worried about her son. He was picked up by the police numerous times for using drugs. He would yell at his mom. He abused their dog. She tried everything and nothing seemed to work. The key word is that *she* tried everything. So I gave her a "God Can."

The mother wrote the following letter:

Dear God,

I can't help my son any more. I give him over to You.

Thank You.

Mom

She folded the letter and put it in her "God Can." The next thing she knew, her son had checked himself into a rehab center!

If you can't, God can.

Not long ago, I had a misunderstanding with a very dear friend. She is like family to me. I was distraught that we were off course. My monkey mind voices began taking control. "Call her up and blame her! Point out everything she did wrong. She's not always there for you anyway!" The voices went on and on and on.

So I got out my "God Can" and wrote:

Dear God,

I can't deal with this situation but You can.

Thank You.

The next day I felt such love and admiration for my friend! We talked and everything was resolved between us peacefully and beautifully. If I had paid attention to those other voices, I would have messed things up and possibly lost a very dear and good friend.

Another friend of mine had her own great experience with the "God Can." She received a call from her brother. He was suicidal. But there she was in Denver, her brother was in another state across the country. There was absolutely nothing that she could do. So she wrote a letter to God and put it in her "God Can." She completely surrendered. A couple of days later, her brother called. He told her that he was doing great. He'd had a profound mystical, spiritual experience, and knew at the core of his being that everything was going to be fine.

Sometimes the monkey mind voices will tell you that you are above all this. They might even tell you that because you are on a spiritual path, you will be able to see everyone and everything in a spiritual light. Let me be the first to tell you it is foolish to believe that you will always be able to bless your enemy and think good thoughts about others regardless of what they do. You will not always have the presence of mind to repeat affirmations, light a candle and incense, pray for the good of someone who angered you, meditate, listen to uplifting music or podcasts or whatever else you do to get centered. What you can do, however, whenever the negativity of those other voices takes control, is surrender. Surrender! Because you can't, but God can.

Surrender to a grand plan and your life will unfold as it's meant to. Step out of the way of your own possibilities seeking to manifest for you. Move out of the way of your own Spirit wanting to work on your behalf.

Did you know that we spend an average of 16 hours a day with our minds bombarded by the thinking of the world? How many of us are in fear because the thinking of the world says that our economy is continually going down, our world is in perpetual turmoil and that disaster of all kinds looms just around the corner?

The thinking of the world does not glorify God. The thinking of the world glorifies all those monkey mind voices, and when we succumb to such thoughts, we inevitably fall short of the magnificence of God's plan for us. We have issues, we have weaknesses, we have fears, we make mistakes. We fall short, we give up—we are human. We forget that we are spiritual beings having a human experience, and that the spiritual part in us is teaching us to let go and let God have His way.

When you hear those voices that judge and criticize, that want you to blame, control and manipulate, voices that create fear and separation from the Divine, go to God. Let Him be your purifier. Let God take from you anything that is less than ideal, less than wonderful, less than worthy of your True Self. Glorify God by letting His will and way manifest in your life.

Because if you can't, God can!

38.

Fast and Feast

Soon it will be Easter, the time when we celebrate the Resurrection. But before Resurrection can occur, there must be a time of releasing our old limiting thoughts and attitudes, which is why we have Lent. The Lenten season offers a wonderful opportunity to consciously rise to a higher state of consciousness.

Ash Wednesday marks the beginning of Lent, a tradition developed by the Roman Catholic Church. Ash Wednesday consists of a Church service where ashes are put on each congregant's forehead, symbolizing that all is temporary and will return to ashes. Of course, Lent was not practiced by Jesus, but came into being because the Catholic Church found it to be a significant step of preparation. Preparation for what? Preparation for the celebration of life, a life that is free and unbound by our own limitations.

Lent lasts for 40 days during which Catholics are supposed to fast. However, too many people turn Lent into a fashionable fad. They give up certain foods, alcohol or smoking—often temporarily. But these are outer behaviors and habits, where as in Unity, we observe Lent from the inside, according to Spirit.

We seek to fast from criticism and condemnation, and instead to feast on brotherly love.

We seek to fast from thoughts of sickness, and instead to feast on God's perfect life.

We seek to fast from thoughts of lack and limitation, and instead to feast on the truth of God's bountiful good will.

It's a time to leave the old behind and step into a whole new existence.

It's a time to welcome a new beginning for you! Lent is when you can be glorified in the new you that is emerging. An annual spring cleaning, if you will. A fast and a feast, to clean out and renew ourselves. As Paul said, "Be ye transformed by the renewing of your mind." [Romans 12:2]

This Lenten season, make it your intention to step into a spirit-filled journey. Make a conscious choice during Lent to measure every thought, attitude and habit against the Christ standard, and it will be a most rewarding time. Make a deliberate and definite effort to eliminate destructive thoughts and emotions. If you get caught up in old habits of negative thinking, ask yourself, "Is this of the Christ?" If not, ask the Christ light to take it from you. Believe it or not, you have been called to this 40-day challenge! Yet, some of you may be having a conversation with God right about now, asking, "Surely, Lord, you don't mean me?"

That very question haunts me from time to time. In fact this last weekend, I was having a gripe session with one of my colleagues and a voice within said, "Surely, Lord, you don't mean me?" Then I thought to myself, "Isn't it amazing how often we criticize in others the things of which we ourselves are guilty?" We do not find our greatest self by a gripe fest, we find our greatest self by holding to the higher thought.

Shortly thereafter, a quote came across my desk, "A great deal of water is flowing underground which never comes up as a spring. You may find comfort in that thought, but you and I must be the water that finds its way up. We must become a spring at which people can quench their thirst." Surely, Lord, you don't mean me? Oh, yes, the Lord means exactly that.

Imagine adopting the Christ mind as it was in Christ Jesus. As we join the ranks of a Christ consciousness, we begin to let go of thoughts and emotions that no longer serve us. In that action alone we serve many.

Now, during this Lenten cleansing process we may at times experience distress, anxiety, guilt or impatience. As spiritual psychologist Jacquelyn Small says, "Remember that these signs of distress are not pathological—rather they are the natural birth pangs of a new consciousness." For 40 days we will go through a cleansing process with some birth pangs. Then we will resurrect ourselves into a new way of thinking, a new way of believing, a new way of perceiving.

Lent can mark a time of great growth for you. A time to give up unproductive habits and attitudes, and replace them with productive ones. Make a commitment this Ash Wednesday to actually work the Lenten season the way it was meant to be. See it with steadfast determination of the Christ standard. Hold to the higher thought until you can say, "Surely, Lord, you must mean me. How may I serve you in the highest way possible?"

Here is a meditation passed down through generations of Unity Ministers that can help you fast and feast as you journey toward your Christ consciousness.

Fast from judging others. Feast on Christ dwelling in them.

Fast from emphasis on differences. Feast on the Unity of all life.

Fast from apparent darkness. Feast on the reality of all light.

Fast from thoughts of illness. Feast on the healing power of God.

Fast from words that pollute. Feast on phrases that uplift.

Fast from discontent. Feast on gratitude.

Fast from anger. Feast on patience.

Fast from pessimism. Feast on optimism.

Fast from worry. Feast on God's fortune.

Fast from complaining. Feast on appreciation.

Fast from negatives. Feast on affirmatives.

Fast from unrelenting pressures. Feast on unceasing prayer.

Fast from hostility. Feast on non-resistance.

Fast from self-concern. Feast on compassion for others.

Fast from discouragement. Feast on hope.

Fast from facts that depress. Feast on ideas that enhance.

Fast from lethargy. Feast on enthusiasm.

Fast from suspicion. Feast on truth.

Fast from idle gossip. Feast on purposeful silence.

Fast from problems that overwhelm. Feast on prayer that sustains.

Amen!

It's All in Your Point of View!

A teacher of mine once said, "Use everything toward your advancement," meaning reframe experiences in your favor. You can choose to see any situation from a viewpoint that brings you joy and peace rather than unhappiness and misery. The facts do not change, but your perspective does, along with your experience.

James Twyman, film producer and author, came to film me for a movie he was doing for Unity. He asked me questions on the fly and I would answer as best I could with the cameras rolling. The whole thing was spontaneous and unscripted. Occasionally, I would wince and cringe at one of my answers. I'd think to myself, "OMG! Now that wasn't exactly the best answer I could have given!" Terribly embarrassed, I would turn to him and say, "Sorry about that. Not sure that was what you were looking for." He would just smile and reply, "Are you kidding? That was perfect! There is so much of this that I can use in the film! Thank you!"

I was judging myself for thinking I wasn't "good enough," while James was complimenting me on a job well done. Same situation, entirely different perspective, which led to an entirely different experience for each of us.

While we cannot always choose the situations we encounter, we can choose whether to regard them with optimism and hopefulness or pessimism and blame. Therein lies our true power and freedom. May you ever know hopefulness and joy!

39.

The Triumphant Power of Easter

The Easter story is more than the account of Jesus' Resurrection. It is a story about you and me, a story about a journey that each one of us takes at some point in our lives.

Spirituality is often conveyed through stories because the part of the brain that understands stories is different from the part of the brain which is analytical and rational. When we allow a story to penetrate our hearts and souls, a kind of alchemy occurs in which the Divine Elixir of Spirit moves in and through us. With the understanding gleaned through stories, we can surrender ourselves to God, allowing the great light of God to touch our hearts, to transform our lives, that we might become more fully who God would have us be. That is what the Easter story is all about.

Imagine if you will, that it is the day of the crucifixion and that the master Jesus is seated by himself in the courtyard. Outside the gates, a crowd has gathered. These are the multitudes that Jesus fed, taught, healed and cleansed on all levels of their being, yet they have gathered to make sure that he is crucified. Authorities have lulled the populace, and they are now convinced that Jesus came to destroy their religion and their God. The goodness they saw and experienced in Jesus is all but forgotten. He can hear them yelling, "Crucify him! Crucify him!"

Have you ever felt like you were being in some sense, crucified? Or have you ever taken part in a "crucifixion" of sorts, as you judged or criticized someone, hurting them deeply? Most of us have.

Let us take a little trip into Jesus' mind and speculate on his thoughts that day.

Alone in the courtyard he remembers the love he has poured out into the world.

He marvels at his aloneness and asks, "With all that I have done why am I here alone? Where are those I taught? Where are those I fed? Where are my friends? Where are my disciples? Have I failed in some way?"

How many times have we felt alone? Going through a difficult time, wondering where our support system was? Once when I was in the midst of a challenging situation, I called my friends and family for help, but no one was around. I then called Silent Unity for prayer support and I was put on hold! I felt very alone.

Back to our story. Jesus ponders the lack of receptivity in the very people he blessed. The louder the noise grows outside, the louder is the clamor for his life, and the greater his astonishment. Not one human being stands beside him.

We may think that in Jesus' hour of desertion and betrayal he stood alone, but he understood his mission and knew, as he prayed, that he was in Divine companionship. Somewhere between his moment of introspection and the moment he is led to the cross, something bigger and greater than his human self steps in that enables him to endure the crucifixion.

Whenever you go through something painful, and you feel like you just cannot endure it any longer, remember that there is something bigger than your human self that will enable you to get through it.

It is at this point in the story, when Jesus takes up his cross and walks through the city of Jerusalem, that many religious belief systems lose their vitality because they get hung up on the cross itself. Easter, at its best, is not a backward look at the cross, it is a forward look to the quality of life we achieve when we surrender to a Higher Power and its Divine plan.

There is no need to get fixated on the cross and yet, we do. We get stuck on blame, despair, guilt, lack of forgiveness and shame. I have a friend who keeps me in line anytime I go into blame, guilt or shame. She reminds me, "Don't die on that cross." She's right! It is truly a waste of time and energy.

Jesus was taken off the cross just as we must take ourselves off our own crosses, and surrender to God's presence in our live, to that something bigger than our human selves. It is a blessed moment when life's adversities give way to such an awakening for it is the end of suffering and the dawn of freedom. It is our resurrection.

Now after Jesus was crucified there was darkness that covered the land, and there was chaos among the people. All you could hear was screaming and shouting. People were caught in hopelessness, confusion and despair, arguing with each other over what was right and what was wrong, fair or unfair. Many were in a state of shock.

We've all experienced chaos in our lives at one time or another. Yet, as science teaches us, beneath the frenzy and disorder lies a pattern, an interconnectedness from which all order evolves. Chaos can give us life-changing lessons—lessons of standing in trust, of releasing our attempts at control and manipulation, opening to new possibilities and insights, letting go of blame and judgment and understanding that God knows exactly what He is doing. He is directing, guiding and leading each situation into its perfect outcome. In the midst of upheaval and uncertainty, we have the opportunity to practice trust in the ever-transforming power of God, to discover the order under all chaos.

Jesus' body is then taken to the tomb, and a great miracle happens in the next three days. Mary Magdalene goes to the tomb only to discover that the stone in front of it has been rolled away and no body is found inside. Today's experts say that to roll that stone away would have taken the energy or strength of four tons. Yet somehow, the light and power of God enabled Jesus to rise from the tomb and to complete his mission and purpose in the Ascension. Once again, Jesus was profoundly engaged in Divine company.

So are you.

The celebration of Easter is not to commemorate an event

which took place two thousand years ago, but to reveal principles so that when we face a world of negativity, of chaos and confusion, we can stand fast in the faith that God is our power and our strength. When we are faced with a challenge, it is imperative that we rely on a Power greater than the circumstance because that is the only way to resurrect and rise above it.

Often we want to rely on the advice and direction of other people and we forget about a Higher Power. We must remember that we can never put our dependence on the outside world, for the world is ever changing, but God is forever the same and forever true.

Jesus said very clearly, "My kingdom is not of this world I am in this world, but I am not of it." [John 17:14-19] Meaning that even though his disciples did not come to his aid, that the people he healed did not testify for him, a Power greater than anyone can imagine enabled him to walk out of the tomb and ascend above all human discord. Jesus' kingdom was not of this world, for he overcame the world. The kingdom of God was within him, as it is inside all of us, and we can rely on this Power always within us.

Everything has a reason. Everything has a mission and a purpose. Everything has a destiny. Imagine if you will, that your life is like that of a bird. A bird is born, with specific characteristics that set it apart from other birds, not knowing the rhyme or reason behind its existence. At a certain point, something within it makes it want to migrate in a southerly direction, even though it doesn't know why or where exactly it is headed. But God knows all of these things, knows the bird's destiny, and assists the bird, without the bird ever knowing that it is being assisted. The bird is always in Divine companionship.

Now, if God has this bird's life and Jesus' life and Resurrection so perfectly orchestrated, wouldn't it make sense to think He's also orchestrated your life perfectly? You are in this world by Divine appointment. Every place, every situation, every relationship in your life, has its unique meaning and purpose. Even those terrible times that you thought you would never get through had meaning and purpose. Every situation that you have ever experienced has had some magnificent purpose or lesson for you.

Once you understand that there is a Divine Intelligence at work at all times and in all places, you begin to open up to the plan that God has in store for you, an incredibly good plan.

As you go about your day, keep in mind these principles:

You are not alone. You are always in the presence of Divine company.

Watch how you crucify people, whether out loud or in your mind.

If you are going through a sort of "crucifixion," release and let go, for there is something greater going on than you can imagine. Trust God's plan for you.

Realize how important you are in the whole orchestration of God.

May the triumphant power of the Easter story rise up within you, and help you prevail over every limiting thought and idea!

40.

Hold On to Your Innocence

Each and every one of us is innocent. That is your original state. God created us to be innocent, and that which is of God does not change. You were born innocent, you have remained innocent, and you will always be innocent. There is nothing that you can do or say or think that can change your eternal innocence in the eyes of God.

That does not mean that we cannot make mistakes. Or that sometimes we aren't locked in by the chains of our own thinking. Or that evil things don't happen. The point is that there are no mistakes God cannot see past. You see, within us there is an innocent Spirit, and there is our personality. Personality is what judges and attacks, personality is what gets in the way of our innocent Spirit.

Michelangelo, when asked how he made a statue, replied that God gave him a piece of marble, within which God had already created the David, the Pieta, and the Moses. All Michelangelo had to do was get rid of the excess marble to free the statue within. So it is with your innocence. You don't create your original innocence, you simply drop everything that gets in the way of it. You free the original innocence that is already within you.

You free your own innocence through seeing it in others. If you attack and judge others, it is impossible to see your own innocence. When you condemn someone because you think they did the wrong thing, then you are wrong even if you are right for there is original innocence in the one that you are so tempted to judge. "Judge not lest ye be judged." [Matthew 7:1]

To refrain from judging is a full time job! As we go through our days, we are constantly tempted to judge. The dominant thought system on planet Earth is one based on the idea that people are guilty. When something untoward happens, we attack with our thoughts, we defend, we judge. In a world obsessed with criticism and shortcomings, it indeed requires vigilance to hold the vision of innocence.

Spiritual progress is about dismantling the thought system that the world has taught us. It is not about learning, it is about unlearning. Every moment we are choosing. We either choose to see the world through our original innocence or through our judgments. If we meet an attack thought with an attack thought of our own, then we are stuck in that hell. It takes the willingness to see beyond what our physical eyes see, and hear beyond what our physical ears hear, to see the innocence in our brothers and sisters.

God responds fully to our slightest willingness. God is not

fooled by appearances. God always beholds us with adoring eyes. When you and I align ourselves and start to see through God's eyes, we see ourselves and others in a whole different light. Judgment is simply not an option.

As a Minister, I am often asked to attend functions and activities as a representative of the Church. At one such function, I found myself in the presence of a man that I had known for some time, but could not stand to be around. There was something about the way that he talked and the way he handled himself that was like fingernails on a chalkboard to me. I call it "grinding my aura." I was angry and judgmental every time he opened his mouth. I noticed this reaction in myself, and I wanted to be free of it, but I just couldn't!

I thought I had better practice what I preach. So I prayed. It is useless to pretend that I—we—don't have angry, judgmental thoughts because that would make us hypocrites. We do! We are, after all, human. What I am referring to is transformation, not denial. My prayer went something like this:

> *Dear God, I am angry. I am being judgmental, but I am willing not to be. Help me. Let me see through Your eyes and hear through Your ears. Help me to see the innocence in this person.*

Well, all of a sudden, his wife walked into the room and berated the man for not hurrying up fast enough to get the car. She didn't want to walk, and why was he making her wait? I watched the man shut down and practically disintegrate before my eyes. I realized that this man was doing the best he could with what he knew. With that, I had compassion for both of them. They hadn't changed. I had changed. God had given me what I needed to see beyond my judgments. The lack of innocence was not in the man, or his wife, it was in me.

Every moment you choose to see the innocence in others, you free yourself. Saying a simple prayer like "God, show me the innocence," is all it takes. You can do this anywhere. When you are at a function, or at work, or even in line at the grocery store, look at the people around you and choose to see their innocence. Do the same thing with your family, your friends, your children, and anyone else who comes to mind. Allow the Holy Spirit to remove from you the temptation to want to judge people.

Now you are back to your original innocence.

Now, you are free.

41.

Your Good: Reborn and Restored

The other day I was reading about an amazing flower, the peony. Peonies are wonderful creations that bud forth in little round hard balls. Now, by a miracle of nature, the only way these buds can open is when certain little ants come and eat away at the peony bud's protective outer shell. A beautiful flower can then emerge.

When I looked at this miracle of nature, I realized that adversities come to us at exactly the moment we are ready to benefit from the strength we gain by learning to handle them. We get exactly what we need, precisely when we need it, to advance us to the next level of our spiritual growth. And we are never given a challenge beyond our ability to master.

A particularly intriguing aspect of the peonies is not only

that it takes a special kind of ant to facilitate their blossoming, but that those ants somehow appear just at the moment when the flowers are ready to bloom. It is a beautiful demonstration of the Truth that God does not take anything away from you without giving you something better in return. There is never any loss without greater gain.

However, if we want greater good to come into our lives, we must make room for it. If we don't do it ourselves, the Universe has an uncanny knack of creating that room for us. For example, you are fired from a job that is no longer for your highest good, only to find another job that is so much better. A relationship leaves your life, only to find that there is a more fulfilling relationship ready to come into your life. The Universe will close all doors except the one that is best for you to walk through.

A friend of mine working in Austin, Texas, with Hurricane Harvey evacuees from Florida, told me of her experience. How inspired she was by an eight-year-old boy, who had watched his neighbors die in the flood and other horrors, yet nonetheless, believed that although he didn't know why all this was happening, he knew God had a reason. That God had helped his family up 'til now, and that God was giving them a new life, a better life. His determined belief and optimism taught my friend about resiliency, forgiveness and the power of love to heal.

Her story reminded me that things are not good or bad in and of themselves. It is what we make of them that determines their worth.

As long as we are alive, we cannot escape loss. Loss is a very real part of life, which comes in many different forms—the loss of a friend, or of a job, the loss of a loved one, or of our finances. There is even the loss of joy, of hope, of peace in our hearts.

Yet God, the very essence of Love, has prepared unlimited, boundless good for each of His children, and that also means you personally. This is one of the great cosmic secrets of the Universe, which has had an electrifying effect for good on the lives of countless people as they have learned and applied it. It can make the difference between success and failure when we are in the midst of loss. However, since this unlimited good is your Divine heritage, it forever awaits your recognition and claim. When loss comes, it is time to call upon the Law of Divine Restoration.

Divine Restoration is that power that is at work to harmonize, balance, refine, readjust and bring forth good even in the midst of loss. In the Bible, each time man has wandered away from his good, or his good has seemingly been taken away from him, good is always restored, even better than before.

In the Old Testament, Joel turns to God after his land was devastated by locusts, drought and famine, leaving him with virtually nothing. Whereupon God tells him [Joel 2:24-26 NIV], "The threshing floors will be filled with grain; the vats will overflow with new wine and oil. I will repay you for the years the locusts have eaten—the great locust and the young locust, the other locusts and the locust swarm—my great army that I sent among you. You will have plenty to eat, until you are full, and you will praise the name of the Lord your God, who has worked wonders for you; never again will my people be shamed."

What is lost will always be restored. If it seems like your good just flew out the window, let it go! For it is good that you have simply outgrown. As Emerson states in his great essay, "The Law of Compensation," something must be taken away from us in order for us to gain. Something must be eliminated to allow the desired good into our lives.

Lately I have given a lot of thought to the teaching, "Give it all up and you'll get it all back." I believe that this is an immensely potent formula for finding joy and peace in one's life. Every time I have put this principle into action, it has worked. Whenever I have to let go of something, God has either given it back to me, or given me something better, or shown me how much better off I am without it. That is the nature of God, the outworking of the Law of Divine Restoration. Our job is to hold fast to the Truth that God is good, and that good is on its way to us. To affirm, "I now call on the Law of Divine Restoration, and my good of the past and the present is now Divinely restored."

When we experience loss, we may want to stay in our story of victimhood, of "woe is me." But being a victim does not allow you to move forward. Many people miss their present blessings because they are still lamenting their loss, and blaming themselves or other people for the loss. They lament, "If that had not happened, then I would be happy today! That experience ruined my life."

Never fool yourself into believing that anyone or any situation can keep you down, unless you let them. There's no reason to give people or experiences that much power over you.

Do you remember *The Road Less Traveled* by Scott Peck? The book opens with the comment, "Life is difficult." When I first read that sentence, I closed the book immediately! I thought, "How could anyone start a book with such a negative statement?

Especially when people are reading it to obtain some sort of spiritual and emotion assistance." But those three words made me sit up and take notice of the truth within the statement: that which is, is.

No, life is not always easy and yes, there can be loss at times, but that doesn't mean that you throw in the towel or resign yourself to the situation. You can instead accept what has happened, and start anew from right where you are. You may see your experience as devastating, but if you affirm Divine Restoration you will experience new growth and new opportunities in your life. Even when you think that there is no way out of the loss that you are experiencing, you are literally surrounded by exactly what you need. Just like the ants showing up at exactly the right time for the peonies to bloom.

When you are experiencing a loss, it is time to go within yourself, not to ask "why," but to ask "what next?" Look for the gain and not the loss. Know that the good of God is present, and you will see that your good will be reborn and restored in God's own wonderful way.

42.

Awakening from Guilt

friend of mine asked me what my next sermon topic would be. I said, "guilt and shame." She said, "Oh good, could you send a copy to my mother?" That reminded me of a bumper sticker that read, "My mother was the travel agent for guilt trips!"

All of us can remember feeling guilt or ashamed about incidents in our lives. There's food guilt, relationship guilt, family guilt, work guilt, money guilt, not following through guilt, making mistakes guilt, past guilt, present guilt, future guilt, telling a lie guilt, being too honest guilt, saying the wrong thing guilt and religious guilt. You name it, guilt comes in many forms and sizes.

In the quest for truth and self-realization, there are few things that we as humans get more confused about or hold on to more tenaciously, than the feelings of guilt and shame. It is not always easy to define a guilty feeling, because guilt is such a disorganized state of mind. We are not even always certain what we are guilty of. We just feel guilty. Or as some say, "I have the guilts."

Why is this?

Every person lives with two conflicting selves within him or herself. I know it's a bummer, but that is the way we are set up. In Unity, we call the two selves the True Self and the False Self. Other people refer to these selves as the Light and the Dark or Shadow Self.

The True Self has never suffered, nor can it or shall it—ever! The True Self consists of everything that is Divine, good and wonderful. It is the God nature within us.

The False Self consists of everything negative within us. The False Self is made up of everything that is an enemy to happiness—attitudes and feelings of blame, anger, resentment, worry, critical judgment. It is the part of us that has caused all of the trouble that we have ever experienced, "The devil made me do it." It is the part of us that has done all of the suffering we have ever experienced. Sometimes it is lurking in the background, sometimes it is full blown, and "up close and personal," causing you all sorts of misery.

Philosophers and spiritual teachers often consider the False Self as our lower nature, or the ego self that lives in illusion—a false personality, not our real Self. This is why a person dominated by his or her False Self does not live their live fully. They may feel hounded by compulsive thoughts of anger, jealousy and resentment, or scared by unrealistic imaginings.

You see, the False Self looks back at the past for what could have been, or what should have been, or what was missed, or what was done that the False Self might get tripped up by someday. The False Self looks toward the future with apprehension, with concern and worry, always planning for a negative future that may never come. When we identify with this False Self and its worries, let it live in us and speak its word through us, we begin to believe that is who we are. But the False Self is not who you truly are!

When you were young, the False Self was not fully formed. You were closer to who you truly are, your True Self, your Light Self, your Divine Self. Can you remember those delightful moments? The experience of your original innocence, when your shame and guilt were not fully formed. Or perhaps you have seen the True Self in a small child, before that child has learned to be fearful and resentful. Jesus taught us that in order to enter into the Kingdom of Heaven, we must first become like a little child, meaning we must fully realize our true innocence. That is your True Self. Since we all possess this True Self, there is great hope for us.

Primitive man controlled his environment with physical power because the False Self believes in overpowering other people. Modern man does much the same thing—or attempts to—with his enemies, be they nations or people or even corporations. But modern man then takes it a step beyond sheer physical prowess. We are not usually so primitive as to take a stick and beat each other over the head. However, we have other "sticks" that we take up, other ways we cause people to be or do what we want so we can be happy regardless of their happiness/unhappiness.

The False Self in us has learned to dominate or manipulate

our immediate environment by controlling friends and family using the emotions of fear and guilt.

Now guilt can come in very subtle ways. For instance, let's say that you and a friend are on your way to the movies, a movie your friend chose. On the way there, you have a conversation that resulted in your feeling getting a little hurt. So you decide to get back at your friend by refusing to enjoy the movie. After the movie, when your friend asks you how you liked the movie, you reply, "It was fine," meaning the exact opposite. After which you subject your friend to the silent treatment.

As a kid I used to say things like, "Mom and dad, you go out and have a good time. Don't worry about me. I'll just stay at home and pet the dog." Fortunately, my parents never bought my attempts to guilt trip them.

However, we do have the power to make others feel guilty. Subtle or not, we have all at one time or another done everything in our power to make another person feel bad. Not only that, but our emotions can uplift or entrap ourselves as well.

One of my favorite stories is that of a Samurai warrior who came to a Zen master for instruction. "Master, do heaven and hell really exist?," asked the Samurai. The Master broke out into laughter. "You?" the Master replied. "You would like to know about heaven and hell? Don't be ridiculous! Just look at you. You're fat, you're ugly, you're uneducated, and you're uncouth! What teacher would invest his time in someone like you?" With that the Master turned his back on the Samurai and ignored him.

The Samurai thought about all the Master had said and felt a deep sense of guilt and shame. "Yes," he thought to himself,

"I am uneducated, I am fat and ugly, and I am uncouth." The Samurai's face turned red, his breath came short and fast. He drew his sword to kill himself. Just as the sword was about to enter the Samurai's body, the Master turned around smoothly and calmly and said, "That, sir, is hell." The Samurai stopped cold and realized the depth of the Master's teaching for him. He saw instantly how he had created his own hell through his shame and guilt. Immediately, he fell at the Master's feet in awe of the moment. The Master looked down at him, lifted the Samurai's head and said quietly, "And that, sir, is heaven."

Your emotions can take you to God or they can take you to hell. They can take you to your True, your Divine Self, or they can take you to your False Self. So if guilt is hell, why do we hold on to it? We live in a society with moral, cultural and behavioral standards, some created by parents, teachers and religions. If you don't live up to those standards or function within them, then you are supposed to feel guilty. I guess it is one way of saying that we care. That if you do something wrong at work, you care enough to feel guilty. If you said something inappropriate, you care enough to feel guilty. There is only one problem with this approach. When you are on this spiritual path, it will not work. You cannot control your outer world through shame and guilt.

Yet many of us still have a guilt we've carried around for a very long time. I had an ancient guilt that lived with me for 20 years. A family member passed away and left me quite a bit of money. If invested wisely, it would have been enough to set me up for the rest of my life. But greed set in, and I chose to invest it all in one stock, because I was guaranteed that this particular stock was going to triple in value very shortly. Well, you can guess what happened. I lost it all and I felt ashamed and guilty for years. Yet what I was doing was a sin—what we in Unity call "Self Inflicted Nonsense" (S.I.N.). It's only after I asked for the spirit of Grace to wash over me that I was able to release my "sin" of guilt and shame.

Now, that's not to say that there aren't times when a little bit of guilt can be good. A little guilt can be beneficial if it makes you get up and do something about the situation. Like making amends to someone and taking personal responsibility. But if you allow guilt to be a predominant emotion, you hamper your ability to live fully and productively in the present and you mortgage the future. You lament how bad you've been, fully convinced that you really are bad. Yet, not one iota of self-limiting guilt will change a thing.

Erma Bombeck said, "Guilt is the gift that keeps on giving." That is so true! All kinds of things happen to us that cause pain and guilt. We don't have to carry this "gift" around with us once it's served its purpose—which is simply to learn from whatever you did or said. You can determine to grow through it. Learning and growing through past behavior is healthy.

When we are in the midst of feeling the guilts we forget that we are Divine. We forget about our True or Divine Self. The Divine Self in us transcends destructive emotions and transforms our world into love. Therefore, when you are in the midst of negative emotions like guilt or shame, it is essential to bring your True Self in. To love that part of you that is lurking in the shadows. It is not always easy, but it is extremely important.

For instance, when you are feeling guilty, stop for a moment. Bring up the feeling of love and project it toward that False Self within you. I guarantee the guilt feelings will dissipate. The

Shadow Side of yourself is calling to be loved, to be embraced. As one of my teachers was fond of saying, "Everything is to be loved. All of it is for loving." That means your False Self, your Shadow Side, too.

When we all put our thoughts and prayers toward God and the spirit of Grace, we can transform our negativity—whatever form it takes—in the twinkling of an eye. Life is too short for us to be paralyzed by guilt. Learn from it. Allow Grace to heal you and restore the sense of your True Self, the Divine within.

What if?

There is a question, one question, that can change how you view your life. In fact, it can change your whole state of being. The problem is we ask the wrong questions. Many times we ask "How did this happen? How did I get myself into this mess? Why is this happening to me? Or why is this person doing this or that?" Whatever it might be, a "how" or "why" question contains you in a restricted state of consciousness. But there's one question that can shift you out of that constricted state; it's "what if?" with a positive spin.

What if? "What if I won the lottery, what would I do? What if I got a new car? What if someone new came into my life? What if I got a new pet?" See, the question "what if" asked positively opens you up to infinite possibility. And the force of all good can come rushing forth to match that frequency. But if you're asking how and why did these things happen, you stay in a constricted state.

So today, ask that one question "what if?" and watch how the force of all good will manifest to match your frequency. You cannot help but have a wonderful day!

43.

The Challenge of Forgiveness

From the moment we are conceived until the day we die, we are vulnerable to the actions of other people. They may disturb or even deeply hurt us. Unfortunately, we also do our share of hurting others. The choices we make impact others, whether we like it or not. We are all so intertwined that no one can make it through life without dealing with forgiveness.

As Alexander Pope, the English poet, wrote in *An Essay on Criticism*, "To err is human, to forgive divine."

Forgiveness is not what happens when someone has done something wrong and you believe that in your spiritual superiority you have the authority to forgive. That is a human delusion, which comes from a place of self-righteousness. On the contrary, forgiveness is a Divine corrective that lifts us above the pain of life and delivers us to higher, sweeter ground.

Most people believe that when you forgive someone, you are doing something for them. The truth is, when you forgive, you are doing it for yourself. Not only are you releasing yourself from bondage, but you are also releasing what you do not want to make room for what you do want. In other words, you are giving up pain, anger, resentment and fear in order to experience goodness, joy, peace and love. When you forgive, *you* reap the benefits.

Can anyone ever forget the 2006 fatal shooting outside of Lancaster County of 10 Amish children aged six to thirteen? A milk truck driver drove his vehicle up to the one-room schoolhouse, got the boys out, barricaded the doors so none of the girls could escape and proceeded to shoot the female children before shooting himself. As if the violence wasn't enough, what people talked about most was the reaction of the Old Order Amish community to the shooter's wife and three children.

Within hours, the Amish community publicly forgave the killer and expressed loving concern for his widow and three children. After burying their own children, the Amish attended the burial of the 32-year-old non-Amish killer, and greeted the widow and her children with hugs and a fund they started for her family. "Your love for our family has helped to provide the healing we so desperately need," the killer's widow, Marie Roberts, wrote the Amish. "Your compassion has reached beyond our family, beyond our community, and is changing our world." ("The Scandal of Forgiveness," *Christianity Today*, January 2007). Yet some people were scandalized by the Amish's love and compassion. "Hatred is not always wrong, and forgiveness is not always deserved," wrote Boston Globe columnist Jeff Jacoby.

Forgiveness doesn't mean you're Pollyannaish about the world or plaster over the cracks in people and history. It doesn't mean that you hang out with or go back to the abuser. Forgiveness looks square in the face of wrong and chooses healing and reconciliation rather than hatred and revenge. As I well know, it can be the hardest thing in the world to do.

I was involved in a situation where it appeared certain individuals' sole purpose in life was tell lies about me and made sure that large groups of people would know about their tall tales. They complained to Unity Headquarters about me, without my being able to defend myself. My initial reaction was to profess my innocence and make them wrong. I wanted to let the world know just how awful these people were. Then I saw someone at the grocery store with a bracelet that had the initials WWJD (What Would Jesus Do?). That changed my entire view of the situation. Jesus would not revel in revenge. Jesus would turn the other cheek and keep on going, meaning, "Leave that alone and follow a Higher way." This proved to be a much freer way for me to live my life!

You don't forgive to change the other person, you engage in this practice to free yourself. As Lewis B. Smedes so wisely said, "To forgive is to set a prisoner free, and discover that the prisoner was you." Every encounter is an opportunity to criticize and judge, or to be compassionate and forgive. Judgment calls for punishment, while forgiveness brings release. Forgiveness is a gift you give yourself through others.

The key to forgiveness is to acknowledge the true innocence in another human being. It does not mean, however, that we let go of our boundaries, standards or principles. Forgiveness doesn't destroy our ability to think or does it make us weak. Rather, forgiveness makes us strong because it brings us into alignment with the wisdom of our souls. We become aware of the steps we need to take in order to create harmony in our lives.

We all make mistakes; mistakes are a way of human life. When you come into a higher way of thinking, you understand that each time you make a mistake, you are provided with an opportunity to do things differently. But many people make the same mistake over and over again, without even realizing that they are making mistakes or hurting others along the way. These people can be very hard to forgive! Yet, as Emmet Fox, the great New Thought spiritual leader, taught, "When you hold resentment against anyone, you are bound to that person by a cosmic link, a real tough mental chain. You are tied by a cosmic tie to the thing that you hate. The one person perhaps in the world, whom you most dislike, is the very one to whom you are attaching yourself, by a hook that is stronger than steel." What a powerful insight!

A woman who had been sexually molested by a family member for most of her childhood was consumed with so much anger and hatred that it prevented her from having a fulfilling life. She couldn't keep a job, her relationships were never gratifying, she was constantly having trouble with finances and her health was poor. Then she came across Emmet Fox's teaching, and realized that she had attached herself to the person she most disliked by a hook stronger than steel. She realized that her unforgiveness was blocking her good, draining her energy. She did not want to live life in that manner anymore.

So every night before she went to sleep, the woman would imagine seeing the innocence and loving essence of the family member. She went beyond their personality into their true self. She asked God to forgive through her, because there were times when she personally could not forgive.

I was amazed by her courage, and further amazed at what began to happen in her life. She looked younger than I had ever seen her. She started her own business. She began a relationship where she was treated like a queen. Her whole life was completely transformed. She was an astonishing example of the power of forgiveness.

You too may have unconsciously hooked yourself energetically to a person or an experience. You may have a long-standing grievance with someone or with an organization. You may be blaming others for your experience. You may feel badly about it. It is draining your energy and you long for some kind of relief, yet you feel stuck in anger and resentment. You do not want to forgive.

Yet, forgiveness is the only way to be free. When Jesus was being crucified, in that most awful time, he demonstrated that there is a place within each of us that can say, "Father, forgive them, for they know not what they do." He saw beyond the personality of those condemning him to their core innocence.

The difference between Jesus and you or me is not that he was created under some special dispensation, but that he acted constantly at the level of his Divinity, while most of the time, you and I act and react at the level of our humanity. This is why, when I find it challenging to forgive, I ask God to forgive through me. This is available to all of us.

If you have long-standing resentments, ask yourself, "When I am on my death bed, will any of these resentments matter?" Even if you were treated horribly at some point, how does it serve you to cling to your resentment? Or if someone acted unkindly, or the house didn't get picked up the way you wanted, or your plans didn't go your way, in the end, do any of these things really matter? Forgiveness is important, for it brings great peace into our hearts and lives. And although sometimes it may be very difficult, the invitation is for us to try.

To try to bring peace into who you are. To try not to separate ourselves from our Divine self through resentment or anger. To try to see the Divine innocence in others. To try to stand for something Higher than what the world might see as justified hatred.

A Course in Miracles teaches, "The Holy Spirit will respond to your slightest invitation." To try to forgive is the slightest invitation that the Holy Spirit needs to respond to you. Watch and be astounded at the power of forgiveness!

44.

Be Pure in Heart

The Sermon on the Mount, one of the most important sermons of Jesus' ministry, begins with the Beatitudes, one of which is:

Blessed are the pure in heart, for they shall see God.

According to New Thought philosopher Emmet Fox, if you actually understand and put this Beatitude into practice, you will experience the new birth of your own Divine nature.

The promise of this Beatitude is nothing less than to see God. To see means spiritual perception, the capacity to apprehend the true nature of Being. It's where nothing is wrong, life is good and you are at peace. You are content and really like who you have become. You have the feeling that God is ever so near and that all is well. That is the true nature of Being. That is who you truly are.

If we want to experience more of our true nature of Being,

how do we get there? By being pure of heart, which means to live your life in integrity. To tell the truth. To no longer blame others for your circumstances. To be accountable for your actions. To keep yourself clean and clear at all times. To be aware and act on the Truth. When we live in integrity, we align with the force of all good. We walk with God.

There once was a wise teacher who gave each of two men a chicken. The teacher told them to kill the chickens where no one would see. The first man went behind the barn and killed his chicken. The second returned after three days with a live chicken. The teacher asked the man, "Why didn't you kill the chicken?" The man replied, "You told me to go where no one is looking, but everywhere I go, the chicken sees."

It is the same in our lives. No matter where we go, someone might be watching. We can deceive others and even our own conscious mind, but everywhere we go, our own inner God-self sees. It's what no doubt prompted Shakespeare to write, "And this above all, to thine own self be true. And it must follow as night the day, thou canst not be false to any man." [Hamlet, Act 1, Scene 3]

Sir Thomas More, Lord High Chancellor of England in the 1500s, was under intense pressure to abandon his code of ethics. He was perhaps the only man in England who stood for his beliefs rather than support a corrupt King. His position, his family and his life were all under threat of death. In a last ditch effort to get More to sign an oath of allegiance to the King, a colleague asked him why he didn't comply "for the sake of comradery." More famously replied that if he went to hell for not following his conscience (by signing the oath), would his colleague join him in hell "for the sake of comradery"?

Every day, we are all given countless opportunities to choose between living in integrity or being out of integrity. To choose between blaming others, or choosing personal responsibility. When we refuse to accept something not in alignment with our integrity, than it can hold no power over us.

Certainly, we live in a world where there are chaotic influences such as media, negative co-workers, arguing friends and family members, and if we are not careful, we can lose touch with our inner truth. So how can we remain a person of integrity? First and foremost, tell the truth.

All of us have lied at one time or another for what may have seemed like good reasons at the time. What we often call "little white lies." But if you feel you must tell a "little white lie," it is better that you say nothing at all. For as innocent as a "little white lie" may look on the outside, it knocks you off balance on the inside, in your Divine nature.

Some years ago, I worked with a counseling client who always arrived 20 to 30 minutes late for his appointments. Every time he would tell me a little white lie—he got tied up in traffic, or there was some sort of emergency, or something happened to his dog, to his car. Finally I said to him, "I think your greatest healing would come from telling the truth and being in integrity with yourself." I had come to realize that he suffered from very low self-esteem, which is why he would lie about things and then beat himself up about lying. In order for him to appreciate the person he was, he needed to start telling the truth, no matter how big or little the circumstance. The man did just that. After a short period of truth-telling, he began to like himself. As his self-esteem increased, people, places and circumstances responded to him in positive ways. He got a promotion at work. His love life greatly improved. He was given opportunities that he would have never imagined. Much good comes from telling the truth.

Another way to stay true to your integrity is to listen to your inner guidance, your inner Truth. Often we hear our inner guidance, and then go promptly in the opposite direction. Unfortunately, if we continue to ignore our guidance, that guidance will eventually be a lot harder to hear.

Whenever you need guidance, ask yourself, "What does my inner Truth say?" Your inner Truth is that knowing from the gut. It will never lead you astray. Sometimes it may not look like the way you think it should, but follow it anyway. Noah, for example, built an arc in the absence of any water appearing anywhere. People thought he was crazy, but he followed his inner truth, which turned out to be "the" truth. When you listen to your inner truth you will always be in the right place at the right time. Stay true to your integrity and follow your inner guidance.

Be true to yourself and you will be at peace. You will be standing in your power. It takes tremendous courage to live in integrity, but without integrity, it is virtually impossible to progress along the spiritual path. Living in integrity will provide you with the most rewarding perspective on life. It will give you the greatest degree of insight and understanding you can possibly have.

Integrity is not a state to be achieved, but rather a state to be recalled. You arrived on this planet innocent, pure, and full of integrity. Only you can realign yourself to your integrity, and when you do, you are truly living in the Light.

Blessed are the pure in heart, for they shall see God.

45.

Discover Your God-Given Talents

L abor Day is a legal U.S. holiday celebrated on the first Monday in September. It was initiated in 1882 by the Knights of Labor to honor the working class and formalized In 1894 by Congress as a legal holiday.

Almost all of us work—at a job, raising a family, keeping a household running or volunteering. Why? Because we need to. Working is a need almost as essential as hunger. It is a way to express yourself in meaningful effort.

It is a way to share with others the energies and talents you possess. Work can bring the greatest form of happiness and satisfaction you will ever know. As Charles Kingsley writes, "Thank God every morning when you get up that you have something to do, which must be done, whether you like it or not."

Luke 2:41-52 states, "You must be about your Father's business," meaning that God is your employer. God gave each of us certain talents and abilities. These abilities are an integral part of our Soul. They make us unique and able to do things that no one else can. God then, put us here for a purpose— to expand and express our God-given talents.

While it is true that we may work for a given company, in a larger sense we are all employed by God. So if by chance, your company job has come to an end, know that you can never lose your real job. Rest assured that God has another place where you can express your talents, which may be even better than your last job. When your faith is in God as your employer, you have a true sense of security that nothing and no one can take from you, no matter what. After all, none of us can look to an institution, an industry or even the government to guarantee our security, for these are ever changing. God is unchangeable.

Sometimes people say, "Oh, I don't have any talent. I wish I did! But I can't sing or write or play an instrument. I'm just an ordinary person with no special abilities." You may even have said that at times about yourself. Nothing could be farther from the truth. You may not realise it, but you have tons of talent, ready to be used and employed.

Webster defines talent as, "The abilities, powers and gifts bestowed upon man; natural endowments thought as a divine trust." We may know that God has bestowed gifts upon each of us, but how often do we think of talents, abilities and gifts as a Divine trust? How often do we use them to add to the well-being of others and ourselves?

Not nearly enough, for the simple reason that we take our

"abilities, powers and gifts" for granted. Consequently, we do not use or appreciate them to their fullest extent. Yet there are God-given talents that we all possess—the talent to serve, to radiate joy, to heal, to learn, to play, to laugh, to grow, to pray, to forgive, to praise and to love among many others. Yet with all these talents, the most important of all is the talent to *do*.

We may recognize some of our talents. We may even think and talk about them, but unless we use our talents, it's as if they didn't exist. When you don't use your talents, you experience contraction or discomfort in your life. Whereas, when you express your talents, you experience expansion, fulfillment and excitement.

Your talent is a gift that comes with the tools to express it perfectly. If, for example, you have artistic talent, you also have within you all the skills necessary to express that talent successfully. Oh, you may want to expand those skills, develop them further, but the basis of those skills are already yours. And the more you use your talent, the more confident and comfortable you become in expressing it fully and freely.

As I was growing up, I lived in my brother's artistic shadow. He was an amazing artist. He won award after award for his art. My artistic attempts were taped to the family refrigerator, while my brother's artwork was framed and hung on the wall. Given the obvious contrast, I never thought I had any artistic talent.

A few years ago, I felt a need, a compulsion, to paint—just for the glory of God. I was astounded at how that need expressed itself. I began painting furniture in funky and wild ways! Then came the bigger surpirse. People actually wanted to buy my eclectic painted furniture! I now have pieces in other people's living rooms, kitchens, offices and dining rooms. Painting in my unique style has become vital to my well-being, as important as breathing.

Every species in this world has a place and a function that is specifically suited to express a certain talent. Some are uniquely equipped for physical work, such as athletics, dance or construction. Some have special gifts for inventing or organizing. Others have creative minds for writing, design or mathematics. I could go on and on.

Any talent you were born with eventually surfaces as a need, as something you must express. Current research on child prodigies, whether they be mathematical wizards, musicians, performers or artists, tells us that these children possess a burning desire to express themselves, to use their unique talents.

If you're not a child prodigy, however, how to you find that special talent, and how do you let God employ it?

Here are some tips:

1. Make a list of things that you love to do.

2. Choose one thing that expands who you are, and that fills you with a sense of excitement.

3. Make a list of the ways you can express this talent in the world.

A friend of mine who did this exercise realized that her talent is organizing. She formed a company to help people get organized. She found that this kind of self-expression breeds self-confidence in herself and in her customers. Another friend loves to work with plants. Her excitement led her to become a landscape architect. Yet another friend discovered that she loves astrology. She immersed herself in the study of astrology and now thoroughly enjoys her work as an astrologer.

Work is a natural vehicle for the expression of talents because we spend so much time at work. It makes absolutely no sense to turn off our abilities and forget our need for expressing our talents 40 hours every week. Whatever our work is, whether we love it or not, we can chose to elevate our experience of work by doing it well with the God-given talents we all have—the talents of love, service and joy. As you practice these, you will find your work increasingly gratifying.

Those of you who do not work in the traditional sense are still employed by God to serve Him and others by expressing your God-given talents. You can't clock out until He tells you to clock out! Your God-employer is more than fair and will reward your efforts. You will never be fired. Even if your work seems menial and unimportant, the knowledge that God is your employer can give you a new feeling of dignity. It releases power within you. It allows you to perform even ordinary tasks with joy and satisfaction.

Employ your God-given talents. When you realize that God is your employer, when you are so happy, free, joyous, prosperous and peaceful, you'll say to yourself, "Why didn't I do this before?" You will hear Him whisper, "Well done, good and faithful servant, thou hast been faithful over few things. I will set thee over many things; enter into the joy of the Lord." [Matthew 25:23]

You will know what He means, because you will already experience the utter joy of fulfillment.

46.

⎯⎯⎯⎯⎯∞∞∞⎯⎯⎯⎯⎯

The Power of Deliberate Intention

It has been said that we are the screenwriter, the producer, the director and the star of our ongoing autobiography.

In the melodrama called "My Life," you have had many experiences—love, romance, heartbreak, loss, marriage, divorce, children, death, jobs, no job, lots of money, no money, health, sickness and on and on. All of these experiences are episodes in "My Life." These dramas' scripts all tend to have the same theme—we're either getting into trouble or getting out of trouble.

No one stars in any of these episodes but you. You are, literally the "star" of your own life! How you show up in these episodes is entirely up to you. I like to use the word "episode," because much like in a television episode, any problem or situation has one guaranteed result at the outset—there will be an end to the problem. For me, that means that I can trust and accept that "this too shall pass." Whatever the situation, it is not here to stay.

Think of a circumstance in your life for a moment. Will the circumstance be just another episode or will you turn it into a full-length big-screen production with a cast of thousands? You get to choose! And just as a screenwriter is able to re-write a screenplay, so can you. You can edit, re-write, change and alter it any way you wish. You can even get rid of characters. However, if you believe that you do not have the power to change your circumstance, then not one word of dialogue, not one scene, not one aspect, can be altered. You are then stuck in the drama of your life.

You see, the beginning of any editing or alteration of the production called "My Life" is to know that it is possible to change something. Some of you may be thinking, "There is no way I can change my script! I am stuck in a predicament I can't move beyond." Believe me, I understand! When I went through the episode entitled "My Divorce," I had the hardest time moving beyond my current reality. My husband had decided he didn't want to be married any more. How could I possibly change anything about that?

So let's dissect this for a moment.

You can change the circumstances of your life by changing your thoughts and feelings about it. In other words, you change the focus of your chosen *attention*. And in that, you are an effortless creator! That being said, where is your "focused attention" and what are you effortlessly creating?

In my divorce episode, my focused attention was on conditions I did *not* want more of. I was afraid of not being able to make it on my own financially. I was afraid that I would never be in another relationship, that men didn't want to be involved with Ministers. And I was ashamed that this was my second divorce. I was therefore effortlessly creating more of what I did not want. Why? Because my thoughts and emotions were immersed, engaged and completely absorbed in the drama.

That is true for all of us. As long as we keep our focused attention on what we do not want, we will continue to effortlessly create the unwanted condition or circumstance in one form or another.

EnlightenedConsciousness.com reported on several recent studies, conducted by three different teams of scientists, which verify what Unity has been teaching for the last 129 years—that our thoughts and emotions do indeed shape our reality!

Unity's teachings on this subject, in a nutshell, are that:

Thoughts create experiences.

Human beings create their experiences by the activity of their thinking. Everything in the manifest realm has its beginning in thoughts.

We are co-creators with God, creating reality through thoughts held in mind.

We create our life experiences through our way of thinking.

[The Biblical reference for these teachings is Galatians 6:7]

Back to the science. In the first experiment, human DNA in a sealed container was placed in one room, while the DNA donor was in another room. The scientists subjected the donor to a variety of emotional stimuli, as well as asking the donor to recall negative and positive situations in their life. Interestingly enough, the donor's emotions affected their DNA all the way in the other room. In the presence of negative emotions, the DNA tightened and constricted. In the presence of positive emotions, the coils of the DNA relaxed and expanded.

In the second experiment, scientists extracted white blood cells from donors and measured electrical changes in the cell's DNA. The donors' DNA was situated in a room several floors below the donors' location. The donors viewed an assortment of news clips and other clips, which elicited different emotional responses from the donors. The donors' emotional peaks and valleys showed up in the DNA as identical responses at the precisely the same time. Even when the scientists separated the donors and their DNA by 50 miles, they obtained the same results—positive expansion or negative contraction of the DNA depending on the donor's emotion.

The third experiment proved something even more remarkable. In order to determine the impact of DNA on our physical world, scientists observed light photons inside a vacuum, into which they'd inserted human DNA. Light photons, a basic unit of nature called an "elementary particle," are a bundle of electromagnetic energy that make up all light, thus make up the world around us. Light photons can be thought of as a scientific way of referencing God-force or Source, Spirit, everywhere present.

When they inserted the human DNA into the vacuum containing the light photons, the scientists discovered the light photons realigned themselves precisely to the geometry of the DNA. With that, these scientists could not help but come to an astonishing realization—if our emotions impact our DNA and our DNA impacts the behavior of the light photons that are the basis of our physical reality, our emotions physically change the world around us.

We create our reality by choosing it with our thoughts and feelings. The focus of your chosen *attention* is what shifts the circumstances of your life, regardless of whether your intention is to have more money in the bank, finding the love of your life or landing the best job ever. Focused attention, however, is not the same thing as wanting to control everything. We often are caught up in thoughts such as, "I want this new circumstance, but it needs to be under these conditions. It has to look like exactly like this. It has to come through this exact channel. And I don't want to lose this other thing or my relationship with that person in the process. If this occurs, then it needs to happen in this certain way."

These thoughts reinforce what we do not want, to the detriment of what we do want. Your DNA tightens and contracts with such thoughts, and since light photons pattern themselves on your DNA, you are simply creating more of what you do not want—over and over again.

So what does that mean?

It means that you can't wait for the lottery to hit in your favor to be prosperous. You must feel prosperous and abundant right now to impact your DNA so you can manifest prosperity and abundance. It means that you can't wait for your healing to have wholeness. You must feel wholeness to impact your DNA for your healing to occur. It means that you can't wait for your relationship to feel love. You must feel in love to impact your

DNA so that your relationship can find you. It means that you can't wait for your new job to be empowered. You must feel empowered first by the thought of your new job!

Doing this requires a tremendous amount of awareness. You can no longer indulge in old negative habits of thought, either with yourself or with others. You must stay conscious and pay attention to who you are being all the time. You can't let any thoughts slip by that will interfere with your desired intention. You can't complain and blame, for example, and expect your positive future to show up.

You must maintain your new pattern of positive and uplifting thoughts for a significant period, so that your entire being can catch up. It takes repetition. It takes will and it takes commitment. But the good news is that it is possible!

Remember, you are the screenwriter, the producer, the director and the star of your ongoing autobiography. The focus of your chosen *attention* is what shifts the circumstances of your life. Intention is a powerful force when allied with chosen attention. Use it well!

Wonderful, Wonderful You!

The day I turned 50 felt totally unreal. Yikes! It seemed that just yesterday that I was in high school. In my head, I think I'm 29 on a good day, and hanging around 40 on my slowest day. I know, those of you over 50 are saying, "Oh! Boo-hoo, Cathy turned 50!" And yes, I realize the number is irrelevant. It's what you decide to do with it that matters. To quote Carol Matthau, "There is no old age. There is, as there always was, just you." Ah! What a great line!

So what can I do with where I'm at? I have a wonderful opportunity to take inventory of who I have become, where I have been and what is ahead. I can see what is important. I can discover things I can let go. What's great is to realize that the days of living from the pressure to please are gone. Gone also are the days of feeling as if I have to sell myself short. As well as the days of being attached to having to be right. Oh, such freedom! As I let go, I look to the future with a bursting desire to be more of who I am becoming, to love more authentically and live more joyously.

Today, no matter how many or few years you've inhabited planet Earth, take time to let go of what can be released and find yourself in a wondrous world of freedom and agelessness where, "There is no age. There is, as there always was, just you."

Wonderful, wonderful you!

47.

Live Attachment-Free

There comes a time in everyone's life when you finally get it, when in the midst of all your fears and what can feel like insanity, you just stop and say "Enough already!"

Enough fighting and crying and holding on to having to be right. Enough trying to change others or hoping that they are going to change. Enough trying to be absolutely perfect or expecting everyone else to be absolutely perfect. Enough taking everything so personally. Enough blaming others for things that maybe you should take responsibility for. Enough complaining and gossiping to others. Enough living in fear of losing a relationship, a job, finances or health. Enough of being the martyr. Enough already!

Finally you get to, "I think I'd better get a life."

To "get a life" means to live deeply every day, from your unique self, rather than merely exist through your days. As

Anna Quindlen, author, journalist and columnist wrote in *A Short Guide to a Happy Life*, "Because unless you know that the clock is ticking, it is so easy to waste our days and our lives." Quindlen, who was all of 19 when her mother died, continues with, "It was the dividing line between seeing the world in black and white and in Technicolor. The lights came on for the darkest possible reason. I learned something enduring, in a very short period of time, about life. And that was that it was glorious, and that you had no business taking it for granted."

When you get to that point, you have an awakening. You awaken to your profound gratitude for the many simple things we take for granted that millions of people on the planet can only dream about—a full refrigerator, clean running water, a soft warm bed and a long hot shower.

So when I say "get a life," I mean a real life, not the manic pursuit of your next promotion, or trying to change your spouse or significant other, or buying a bigger house, or living each moment according to social media. No one ever said on their deathbed that they wished they'd spent more time at the office or that their spouse had taken out the garbage more frequently, or that they wished they'd had that darn face-lift!

It is so easy to waste our lives, our days, our minutes on being mad at someone, or disappointed that our plans didn't go the way we wanted them to, or take something personally, or hold onto the past and blame someone for past actions. It is so easy to take for granted the pale new growth on the spring trees, the bright shine in a child's eyes, the loving touch of your partner, or even the excitement of a thunderstorm. It is so easy to take *life* for granted.

A few years back I went on a canoeing trip. The first day was spectacular. The sun was shining, the water was smooth and easy. We just relaxed and let the river take us where it may. That night we enjoyed camping under the stars. The next day we got into our canoes and noticed some nasty looking clouds hanging over us. As we continued to go down the river, the water got rougher and rougher. Suddenly, a downpour blasted from the skies the likes of which I had never seen. The water became treacherous. Without warning, our canoes capsized, and our tents, sleeping bags, clothing, and food were pitched into the water! We all swam vigorously trying to save the canoes and our supplies. But not all of it was recovered.

We were able to make it over to the side of the river, where we waited for the storm to pass. When evening came, we set up camp with the one tent we'd managed to salvage. We were wet, cold, hungry and uncomfortable. The next day the sun was shining, and we made it back to civilization. As I was sitting at the airport, waiting for my flight home, I realized that my perception of things was different. I had just been through an experience that helped me to appreciate in a whole new way.

I could appreciate life. I could appreciate people just for who they were, without judgment or expectation. My world suddenly was divided into a "former life" and an "after-the-river life." My "former life" consisted of taking things for granted, not really being aware of the here and now. Living on a constant schedule, and feeling guilty if things didn't get done. My "after-the-river life" consisted of simply being and enjoying what was.

As I waited for my plane, an announcement came through the PA that our departure was going to be delayed by half an hour. I watched as people panicked, calling to rearrange schedules, getting angry and irritable over the delay.

Then my all-time favorite airport moment occurred. A man approached one of the airline personnel at the desk, and said, "I need to be on that plane and on my way to California. Now." The airline representative replied, "Well, sir, right now there is nothing that can be done about that. If you will just take a seat, we will keep you informed on the status of the plane." The man said, "Excuse me. Do you know who I am?" The airline representative looked at him, grabbed the microphone, and said, "May I have your attention, please. Does anyone know who this man is? He doesn't seem to know." Many times we get so caught up in our own stuff that we forget how entertaining life can be!

To be at peace, to enjoy simply being and appreciate all that happens in our day-to-day, can happen more easily when we understand that we create much of our suffering by our attachments, by the demands and expectations we make of ourselves or others. The second Noble Truth in the Buddhist tradition is that the origin of suffering is attachment. An attachment is defined as an expectation, a demand, or wanting someone or a circumstance to be a certain way, and getting upset when it doesn't happen.

Our craving, our clinging, our holding on to, our wanting things to be different, can lead to a dissatisfying life filled with thoughts of blame or shame. We don't realize the small ways in which we attach unnecessarily to whatever it is we want—wanting your partner to express their love for you in a certain way, or wanting a particular parking place, or being irritated because your friend was late, or wanting your boss to encourage you more, or wanting it to rain/not rain. So many of the demands in today's world could come under the heading of "Fill me up," "Give me what I want," "Take care of me," "Validate my feelings." And when we don't get what want, we get upset— because we were attached to a specific outcome.

The more we have a mind full of expectations, the less we are free to simply be and enjoy the world around us. Being in the present moment happens when we let go of our attachments. A simple example many of us have experienced is "the date." Let's say that you have a date for Friday night and you begin to fantasize how you want it to look. If you're a woman, you're probably thinking that you are going to a nice cozy, romantic place. Your date may even bring you some flowers. Perhaps you'll go dancing afterward. You've definitely set up an expectation of how you think the date should go.

Friday night comes around, and your date shows up at the door and says, "You know, I've got these basketball tickets. I thought we would go to the game and have some hotdogs and beer while we are there." Well, you're shattered, because you had a well-developed totally different expectation of the date. Now if you didn't have that expectation, you'd simply say to yourself, "Let's see what happens. What really is the priority here?" That's easy! The priority is to have fun and get to know each other better. Now you are not trying to control anything, rather you are open to wherever the moment may take you, open to the possibilities of a higher plan.

One way to recognize your attachments is to notice when you are sad, irritable, upset, disappointed or judgmental. Underneath those feelings you may have an attachment to something being different than it is. We live in greater peace and harmony when we let old attaching behaviors go, when we look at a situation and say, "This has come to bless me," instead of "I want it my way!" For then we will find the blessing and life takes on new meaning.

This is not to say that you should remain passive and just let life happen to you. Instead, surrender your attachment to those situations, events and persons over which you never really had any control anyway. Now you are adaptable to what happens in your life. You can adjust more easily to situations and enjoy greater peace and harmony.

You realize that "what is" is only a temporary phase that evolves almost immediately into "what was." When you let such attachments go, you can truly see that God is with you, and that the whole Universe stands with you, healing you, loving you and comforting you at all times. When you are in God's presence, there are no demands or expectations. God loves you precisely as you are.

Let go of your attachments, your demands and attempts to control, be present and enjoy this glorious life God has given us!

48.

I Have A Dream

If you were told that you had the power to make one change in your life, one adjustment to your thinking, and in so doing you could achieve any dream you desired, would you make that change?

If you were told that by merely surrendering something that you have held dear and clung to most of your life, but that something is the cause of all your problems, would you surrender that something?

If you were told that by merely surrendering the cause of all your problems and then making that choice to readjust your thinking and in so doing, that you would become the person that you always dreamed of being, would you do it?

The thing that you would be asked to surrender is your suffering. You would be asked to give it up—to stop being a pain factory, not only the pain you inflict on yourself, but on others as well.

You see, we manufacture all of our pain inside of ourselves. It does not come from outside ourselves. Certainly, we have been taught that people bring pain and suffering to us in truckloads, but that is untrue. We manufacture it ourselves.

Most people attempt to live their lives from the "outside-in." They feel that they cannot manifest their dreams because they believe they are victim to outside forces. And yet, the great truth taught by mystics throughout the ages is that life is lived from the "inside-out." The whole Universe is concentrated at the point where you are. It stands behind you with its full resources, forever.

It can be said that there are two types of people in the world:

1. Those who choose to believe in their dream, live their dream, and make their dreams happen from the inside out.

2. Those who have forgotten how to believe in their dreams, or even create what they want, because they have allowed outside influences to be their obstacles.

Those who live for their dreams are the creators, the initiators; they are vibrantly alive. They are the people around whom we feel energized, healed, nourished and appreciated. They are the people who move the world along, lifting normality out of inertia and into action. Martin Luther King was such a man. Even unto this day, he has lifted millions of people to believe in his dream and make it possible. He heard and responded to the inner call of his dream, and he stood for what he believed. A great example for us all.

What is your dream? It doesn't matter how little or big it may be, there is no dream that is beyond our ability to accomplish.

God would not plant a seed in your mind if He didn't plan to give you ways to help it grow into manifestation. God is not a sadist, if anything he is a philanthropist! God gives you incredible ideas. It is what you do with them that counts. God did not intend for any of us to be stagnant in life, or for us to cripple ourselves with ideas of limitation or fear.

Let us consider for a moment what someone might believe that prevents him or her from being all that they want to be—lack of skill, lack of money, too young or too old, not enough physical energy, not smart enough, lack of support, etc. But these are not reasons for failure, they are *excuses* that we've all entertained in one form or another at some time. However, not one of these circumstances has the power to withhold our highest good from any of us.

Alan Cohen, author of many inspirational books, tells a wonderful story about a woman who decided that it was time to clean out her fishbowl. Unable to find a container in which to put her two goldfish, she filled up the bathtub and put them in there. After the woman finished cleaning the fishbowl, she looked in the bathtub only to find a very thought provoking behavior—the two goldfish were swimming around in one little corner of the bathtub, in a circle no bigger than the fishbowl.

In many ways, we humans behave no differently. We develop our patterns, our habits, our false beliefs, and when we are given the opportunity to discover a new and freer dimension, we don't. We prefer to stay in our tiny little corner of the world, though it offers us little joy, a lot of anxiety and no expansiveness. We need to step beyond our fishbowl and see that there is a whole bathtub waiting for us.

Many times when we go beyond the fishbowl, it seems illogical to those around us. They may try to convince us not to do so and have all sorts of reasons on why our behavior makes no sense: "Oh, you're just going through a phase," "No one ever made it happen that way," "Your hormones are acting up."

But if we listen to the opinions of others do we still have our dream? Why would you give up your most cherished and important aspirations and settle for less? Do you have a reason to get up every morning, or have you surrendered your personal destiny to conform to the pack? That is what happens when you live from the outside-in.

When fishermen pull up crab traps and put the crabs in a bucket, they don't put a lid on the bucket because as soon as one crab tries to get out the others pull it back down. How many times do we let the opinions of others push us back down? When someone has the courage to believe in themselves, to push past the opinions of others, to push past fears and self-doubt, they succeed not only for themselves but also for you and me and for everyone who needs the strength to go all the way. That determination can make all the difference.

Dr. Glenn Cunningham was one of those people who did not let seemingly impossible obstacles get in his way. As a child, he was in a very bad fire at his school. He managed to survive, but remained crippled. Throughout his life, Cunningham was determined to not only walk again but to run again. He kept working at it day after day. One day it was announced on the news that a man ran a mile in four minutes—the fastest mile ever run in the whole world. That man was Dr. Glenn Cunningham.

But the most amazing thing is that the week after the first four-minute mile was run by Dr. Cunningham, six more people broke the four-minute mile. Those people had no more potential that week then they had the month before. What they had was more *belief* because someone else did it before.

In *Creative Visualization*, Shakti Gawain speaks to the tenets of quantum physics, "Energy of a certain essence, speed or vibration tends to attract other energy of a similar vibration or speed." Your beliefs, which you may regard as without physical effect because they do not have mass or weight, are in fact forms of energy that have a great deal of effect. Every thought or belief that we have holds the power to act like a magnet. It draws whatever forms, shapes, ideas, energy and even people of similar vibration that will help make that thought a reality. The greater the intensity of your beliefs or thoughts, the stronger their magnetic field or drawing power. This was well understood by many spiritual masters. As the Buddha said, "With our thoughts we make our world."

Don't let false beliefs of lack or limitation keep you from creating the kind of life you want. Listen to the voice of God within you, the voice of truth that says, of any such negative thoughts, "What is that to Me? Come now and follow Me." When you are faced with obstacles, whether in your mind or in the world, ask yourself, "Is my obstacle bigger than God? Or is God bigger than my obstacle?" Remember, God would not plant a seed in your mind if He did not plan to give you ways to help it grow into manifestation.

You have within you what it takes to become the person that you always dreamed. Within you are seeds of greatness. There is something that you have to offer the world. So bring your dream into fruition and know that your dream is none other than God's dream for you.

With God, all things are possible!

49.

Free to Be the Real Me

There is a type of insanity that plagues many people. These individuals are fully capable and very intelligent, yet they tend to create lives that don't work very well for themselves—live in which they are quite miserable. Nonetheless, they think that everything is just fine; it's just the way things are.

The kind of insanity I am talking about is the kind that makes one forget about God. It starts with the number one addiction on this planet: control. We want to control people to be the way we want them to be. We want them to do what want we want them to do, and to stay the way we want them to stay. We want to control circumstances, situations and even institutions.

Those who are addicted to control will usually pray to God telling Him what to do. But God can only work for us as long as He can work through us. God can't very well work through us when we are meddling and trying to fix, enable and control.

Do you remember your first love? Mine was Mark*. I thought he was the most spectacular human being I had ever seen. He was handsome. He was the quarterback of the football team. He was romantic. He was nice. He laughed at my jokes. He could do no wrong. He was the guy for me—until the day he announced to me that he was leaving me for Ann*, a cheerleader. I was devastated.

My mom said, "Honey, detach! It's either Mark or somebody better." "Oh, no, mom" I cried; "There is no one better than Mark. He is the only one for me." With that, I began my very brief vocation in stalking. I walked by his house constantly. I called continuously. I wrote anonymous letters regularly. I prayed unceasingly for God to bring Mark back into my life. I was insane. I was suffering from control-insanity.

But that experience was my first profound lesson in detachment. Both my grandmother and my mom convinced me that if I just placed this situation in the hands of God, something really good was going to happen. They reminded me that the Universe knows what it is doing; that when we stop trying to control events, they fall into a natural order. We can relax while a Power much greater than ourselves takes over, and does a much better job than we could have done. My mom and grandmother drilled into my head that I must trust the Power that holds the galaxies together to handle any circumstance in my life.

So even though it was tough—very tough—to let God take over, I detached from the situation, surrendered control, let Him lead and had faith that God knew how to handle my life.

I remember how freeing it felt. Soon after, I met my second love—and Mark was history.

I am human, so this is a lesson that I have had to return to throughout my life. It's not something I learned once and as a result, never ever tried to control anything again. Think about how freeing it is to not always have to be in control. If you detach from how you think things should come about, you will always find freedom. Now this doesn't mean that you become lazy and do nothing, rather it means you follow a Higher Order to things. It doesn't mean that you do not co-create through your own thoughts. It simply means that you let go of the *how*.

Often, we don't believe that there is a Higher Order to things. We believe more in our doubt. Doubt is bred in the mental state of attachment or the emotional investment in an outcome. Doubt shows up when we pray, "God, I've got to have *this* job, or *this* relationship, or *this* house, or *this* way of living." When we have a fixed idea of how things should be, and we believe we have to do it all ourselves in order to receive those things, insanity takes hold and we lose our freedom. Instead, allow Divine Spirit to flow through you to do the work. You don't need to rely on your personal power! In other words, release your personal efforts to make things happen and put the process into God's hands. This is what "having faith" means.

A woman I know wanted a certain kind of house. She prayed about it and visualized it. She was clearly focused on the kind of house she wanted. The woman drove around to various neighborhoods, talked to everyone who might be helpful, and then put her current house in order, ready to sell. After six months, she found a house that wasn't exactly what she wanted, but it was close enough. Since she wanted her dream house now, she was willing to settle for something less. In her impatience, she asserted her will over Divine Will.

After the home inspection, the woman realized the house was all wrong for her and she had to call off the deal. She found another house she absolutely loved. She put in her bid that was accepted, but at the last minute the owner decided to rent rather than to sell. Once again, she was very disappointed. Finally, she decided to give it over to God and allow Him to do his work. She asked for Divine Will to take over.

The next day the woman was reading the newspaper and an ad for a property seemed to just leap off the page and catch her attention. She called the realtor and they went by to see the house. Two hours later the woman made an offer and it was accepted. The house was everything she wanted in the perfect neighborhood.

You see, the process of life is a spiritual one governed by an Invisible Power. When we are in alignment with God and His ways, we know that no matter how things look in the moment, the final outcome will be something good.

Surrendering to God can be tough because it pushes against our fears, confronts our need to control and forces us to release into the hands of God the details of our innermost dreams and desires. Surrender asks us to believe that all will turn out well in spite of appearances.

In Zen Buddhism, there is a concept called the "Zen Mind," or "Beginner's Mind," which says the mind should be like an empty rice bowl. If it's already full, the Universe can't fill it. If it's empty, it has room to receive. The "Zen Mind" teaches that when we think we have things all figured out, we're not teachable and we can't receive our highest good. Detachment, surrender and letting go are the process of emptying the mind.

Similarly, Jesus said we are to become like a little child [Matthew 18:2-4 NIV], "He called a little child to him, and placed the child among them. And he said, 'Truly I tell you, unless you change and become like little children, you will never enter the kingdom of heaven.'" Little children don't think that they know what everything means. Little children ask someone wiser to explain to them.

We are like little children who don't know, but we think we do. I remember hearing another Minister give a sermon and thought to myself, "This is boring. I already know this stuff." Then I heard a very profound statement, "A wise person doesn't pretend to know. They empty themselves to be filled by the experience." With that, I realized that I had been robbing myself of a unique opportunity. So now, when I listen to another speaker, I listen as if it were the first time I've ever heard the principles being discussed. And I learn something new and interesting every time.

When we admit that we don't know, we step back so the Higher Power within us can step forward to lead the way. Jesus clearly distinguished between God Power and human power when he said [John 14:10], "It is not I, but the Father within who does His works."

When we are busy trying to have everything go our way, we are not connected to our Source. We often give our power over to things other than God. We may give our power over to our lovers, our bosses, friends, food, alcohol or even self-pity. When we give our power to circumstances or people other than God, our lives seem unmanageable and insane. We wonder, "What's a nice person like me doing in a life like this?"

Myrtle Fillmore, the co-founder of Unity wrote; "Rest your mind and heart and emotions and body in God. When you are truly thinking God, you cannot struggle to do anything. It is when you are thinking from the little self (ego) that you struggle and see nothing but darkness and grief and failure. No one, not even God, can change you or your circumstances as long as you insist upon coming from this little self."

Free yourself from always having to do it yourself. Free yourself from having to be in control. Put your dreams in God's hands and let Him do His incredible work. God will continue to work His magic on your behalf, even while you are sleeping. "Agree with God first and be at peace, thereby good will come to you." [Job 22:21]

As you go about your day, surrender your will. When you do, you will be reminded that a much greater Power than your own is at work. The "behind the scenes" Power of the Universe, of God is organizing everything into perfect order on your behalf.

*Names changed to protect privacy.

50.

Ask and Ye Shall Receive

A story dear to my heart is how Tony and Rosa Bella Della, that wonderful couple, met. So, here goes.

Some years back, Rosa Bella Della came to our Church in Ventura. She was visiting from Little Italy in San Diego. After the Sunday service, she went up to one of our Prayer Ministers and asked for prayer. Rosa Bella Della said, "I need some prayer. I want a good man in my life. I'm so tired of being lonely, and I no longer want a loser and a disappointment for a boyfriend! I don't like that kind of man. And…"

The Prayer Minister put up her hand to interrupt her, and said, "Um. Let's stay in the positive, shall we? Jesus said, 'Everything that you ask in prayer and believe, you shall receive.' If we ask in prayer today for your wonderful relationship can you trust enough to be a good receiver?" "Oh yes!" exclaimed Rosa Bella Della, "I am so ready for a good man."

With that, Rosa Bella Della and our Prayer Minister prayed. Then, the Prayer Minister said, "Now, Rosa Della Bella, I would like to invite you to do the most difficult thing that can be asked of anyone in our culture. Don't try to figure out how this will come about. I invite you to approach your wonderful soon-to-be relationship with open hands and an open heart. It's not about any effort you might make, but about receiving. Can you do that?" "Oh yes!" Rosa Bella Della said, clapping her hands with glee, "I will be a good receiver!"

Rosa Bella Della gave her prayer request over to God and left our Church that day feeling so positive, she practically skipped out. Well, she would have, except that she was afraid of tripping in her very high heels.

Now here's the deal As soon as you give your request over to God, Divine Intelligence, the Universe, It knows who, It knows what, It knows when! And so It knew who that perfect person was for Rosa Bella Della—Tony, who lived in Florence, Italy. Talk about a perfect match made in heaven! But wait a minute. Rosa Bella Della didn't live in Florence, she lived in San Diego. How was that ever going to happen? How were they going to meet? Ah, but for Divine Intelligence there is always a way! Divine Intelligence doesn't even see obstacles.

So Rosa Bella Della goes about her business just being a good receiver. She gets a call one day from a friend who says, "Hey girl! Guess what? I won tickets to Cirque-du-Soleil in Las Vegas next month, and I have free passes to the after-party with the cast. Wanna go?" Of course, Rosa Bella Della says yes.

Meanwhile, a whole ocean away, Tony had also been pray-ing for a relationship. Nothing was happening, so finally he gave up. He said, "It's going to be what it's going to be." Then Tony's brother said, "Hey Tony! My wife, Lucia, doesn't want to go to Las Vegas in America with me to see our cousin, Vinni. You know, the one who's a trapeze artist in Cirque-du-Soleil. You wanna go with me?" Actually this was a scheme in which Tony's whole family conspired, to get Tony out of his doldrums. Tony said, "Alright, I'll go."

The next thing we know both Tony and Rosa Bella Della show up in Las Vegas attending the after-party with the cast of Cirque-du-Soleil. It's wall-to-wall people. Tony and Rosa Bella Della are just inches apart, but they are unaware of each other. Tony goes out to the balcony to get some air. Few people understand his Italian accent, which makes him feel uncomfortable and very out of place.

Out on the balcony there are dessert carts, and on one of the carts is a beautiful display of apples stacked in the shape of a pyramid. Rosa Bella Della walks out to the balcony. She is famished. She sees the apples, takes one and the whole pyramid of apples start to fall! Rosa Bella Della flings herself over the cart to prevent the rest of the apples from falling. She notices Tony standing there, staring out at nothing, and calls out, "Excusa-me, can you helpa-me please!" Hearing her accent, Tony turns and cries out with joy, "You're Italian!"

Well, needless to say, sparks fly, laughter bubbles up, and smiles spread from ear to ear. Tony and Rosa Bella Della spend the next 48 hours getting to know each other, texting their friends, "I met the person of my dreams!" A year later Tony moves to San Diego, they get married, and they are living happily ever after.

That is how it works! That is how you and I have been creating miracles our entire lives.

God, the Universe, Divine Intelligence, brings us our manifestations through the path of least resistance, which is not what's easiest for the Universe—whose possibilities are infinite—but what is easiest for *you* to allow. What is easiest for you to accept as a deliberate receiver. We know how to ask, and we know how to trust in God. The part of "Ask and thou shalt receive" that hangs us up is the word "receive."

"Receive" is a verb. It is an action word. The first action, step one, that needs to be taken in order to receive is to be a welcoming presence to how the Universe delivers. God, the Universe, Divine Intelligence, will deliver manifestations in the form of insights, hunches and serendipitous coincidences. A series of next steps.

For example, for the Universe to bring you together with just the right people at just the right time, it may orchestrate a delay in traffic. When you're a good receiver, you don't get mad about being in traffic, you just go with the flow. That delay may mean that at the precise moment you walk into Home Depot, you're chosen for a free transformation of your yard! If you'd walked in a minute earlier or a minute later, some other person would have been the lucky recipient of the yard redo.

Or you may have a strong hunch, an almost overwhelming urge, to go and buy a lottery ticket, even though you never, ever, buy lottery tickets. But this day, for some reason, you really think you should. Just this one time, you go ahead and buy one. Guess what? It's a winner.

Notice how this entire process depends on your being a

welcoming presence, both in terms of receiving guidance and of listening to your intuition and hunches. Because if you don't listen, if for instance, you got upset about being in traffic and were a grouch, such that vibrationally speaking, you weren't a match to the Home Depot yard-redo possibility, well, you just missed a chance at having your yard transformed. Except you wouldn't even know it. Which would be sad.

The process of deliberately receiving the life you want depends on your ability to pay attention to the signs the Universe is giving you, and to follow through with what's called "inspired action." Sometimes, inspired action is walking out onto the balcony of an after party, where we "just happen" to meet the love of our lives. Sometimes, inspired action is to wait patiently for the Universe to do its job.

Inspired action is moving with the energy already in motion, as opposed to taking action in order to *make* something happen. Forcing the issue, if you will.

When you take inspired action:

> *You get an impulse or an idea to do something, which comes to you easily and naturally.*
>
> *Inspired action steps make sense. You don't have to justify them, they just feel right.*
>
> *You feel energized by inspired action.*
>
> *You make a lot of progress very quickly, and things happen with very little effort.*
>
> *You allow the Universe to orchestrate events. There is no control on your part.*

When you take "uninspired" action:

> *You spend a lot of time trying to figure out what actions to take.*
>
> *You feel frustrated and overwhelmed. There's just so much to do!*
>
> *You feel tired and depleted. It really feels like "work."*
>
> *You are continuously stopped by roadblocks. Something is always getting in the way.*

Bottom line: inspired action feels good. You're leveraging Universal energy so things just line up for you, it's easy and graceful. Action taken from a place of impatience, from a place of fear, as in "It won't happen fast enough, there's something I should be doing!" is frustrating. It's no fun. You make little progress and it's really, really hard.

Just like with Tony and Rosa Bella Della, the Universe has the power to line up all the perfect components in order to easily bring you what you desire. You don't have the knowledge, the tools or the resources that the Universe has. Why would you try to do Its job?

Therefore, it's not so much about *thinking* your way through life, as it is *feeling* your way through. If something feels right, pay attention. It's something you'll probably want to do, even if you can't logically justify your actions. If something feels wrong, be careful. Very, very careful. Even if it looks good on paper, your intuition is giving you a message of caution. I'm not suggesting you completely turn off your rational mind, but rather that you consider your feelings as equally valid, if not more so.

Ask, believe and be a good receiver! Be a welcoming

presence. And prepare to be amazed at how and where God, the Universe, Divine Intelligence, in Its infinite wisdom, leads you.

From Facebook to Gracebook

About a month and half after my dog Bob passed away, I announced his passing by posting a picture of him on Facebook. I was deeply touched by the kindness and caring of everyone's comments of love and compassion. Their messages made me feel better when I needed it the most.

In the past, I have been known to knock Facebook and the mishmash of posts—from pictures of root canals, to someone's latest pizza pig-out, to some sales frenzy. But with the Facebook response to Bob's passing, I learned a valuable lesson. In that moment I renamed Facebook to Gracebook; a vessel for the force of love to bring healing and comfort to others. *A Course in Miracles* tells us, "Miracles are performed by those who temporarily have more for those who temporarily have less."

On any given day, you may need a miracle or some act of kindness that I can supply for you. The next day I may need some kindness that you can supply for me. As English novelist George Eliot asked, "What do we live for, if not to make life less difficult for each other?" We can be the force of kindness and generosity any time to those in need by sending our loving thoughts to them. We can treat each other with compassion, because peace and love start right where we are.

Let's be kind to one another. Show at least one act of kindness today and watch it spread from one heart to the next.

51.

Maybe Christmas Means a Little Bit More!

I love Christmas. I love Christmas stories, Christmas songs. I love the Christmas TV specials. I even love the Christmas TV commercials! I love them so much I usually begin watching Christmas movies during Thanksgiving week. One of my all-time favorites is the animated classic Dr. Seuss' "The Grinch Who Stole Christmas."

In particular, I love this poem:

> *"Christmas came from Whoville*
> *without ribbons or tags.*
> *Christmas came from Whoville*
> *without boxes or bags.*

Maybe Christmas doesn't come from a store.

Maybe Christmas means a little bit more."

I think Dr. Seuss was a modern day mystic for both children and adults alike. His story is not only a fun one, but its message is spot-on: "Maybe Christmas doesn't come from a store. Maybe Christmas means a little bit more."

In 2 Corinthians 9:15, it states, "Thanks be to God for his immeasurable gift,"— immeasurable meaning invaluable, measureless, of great value, costly, precious and priceless.

Every year we hear the story of the three wise men bringing their gifts of gold, frankincense and myrrh. We are told that the wise men walked for two years before Jesus was even born, that they walked for thousands of miles, searching for the Christ child, carrying their gifts of gold, frankincense and myrrh.

Were the glittering gold, frankincense and myrrh the invaluable gifts of Christmas? Or was it their walk that lasted for more than two years that was the priceless gift—the gift that the wise men gave of themselves?

Isn't this what Christmas is all about— discovering what it means to truly give of oneself, as the wise men did? Discovering what it means to give of yourself in love to another? "Maybe Christmas doesn't come from a store. Maybe Christmas means a little bit more."

The invaluable gift is always the gift of one's self—the giving of yourself through kindness and thoughtfulness and being completely in loving presence for those that are right in front of you.

The Dalai Lama, whose religion is kindness, wrote, "I

believe that if you stop to think, it is clear that our very survival, even today, depends upon the acts of kindness and thoughtfulness of so many people. Right from the moment of our birth, we are under the care and kindness of our parents. Later in life, when facing the sufferings of disease or old age, we are again dependent on the kindness of others. If at the beginning and end of our lives we depend upon other's kindness, why then in the middle, when we have the opportunity, should we not act kindly toward others?" (in the Preface to *The Power of Kindness*, by Piero Ferrucci)

The consciousness of kindness and thoughtfulness is one of the principles that makes your life meaningful. Kindness is one of the great sources of your lasting happiness and joy. Kindness always boomerangs back to you.

How does that work? Well, it is a scientific fact that all things are composed of energy. We know that cells break down into molecules, molecules into atoms and atoms into pure energy. The entire Universe is one flowing stream of vibrating energy. Even though it looks like we are each individual and separate, as energy beings we are all in reality totally interconnected with each other and with everything.

This is why it is impossible to hurt someone or thing without hurting ourselves—why it is impossible to judge someone without it affecting yourself. On the flipside, you cannot help someone without helping yourself. All things being connected, every act of kindness causes a reverberation of positive energy that is felt by the entire world. No matter how large or small your loving action may be, it reverberates to our fellow brothers and sisters on this planet. Your positive energy is valuable to all.

So yes, "Maybe Christmas doesn't come from a store. Maybe Christmas means a little bit more."

"Random acts of kindness" is a catch phrase that has become trendy in recent years. While these "random acts" are good and positive, why would one desire to do acts of kindness "randomly"? The word "random" suggests that the acts of kindness happen on a lottery basis. Instead, for greatest positive energetic effect for the entire world, one should practice continuous acts of kindness. Everyone should be kind to everyone and everything else (animals, the environment, etc.), continuously.

With this in mind, the Golden Rule takes on an even deeper meaning. You realize that by practicing loving others without exception, unconditionally, and truly loving yourself, you come into alignment with the most powerful vibrational energy of all. You come into alignment with love.

One Christmas a very dear friend of mine cleaned out her closet of designer clothing and jewelry with me in mind. She said to herself, "Oh, this would look good on Cathy. I think I will pass it along to her." Then she presented them to me with loving kindness and thoughtfulness in her heart. When I received all the goodies she gave me, I could feel that what she really gave me was the gift of herself, her unconditional love and kindness. I wanted to pay it forward.

I cleaned out my closet and asked Spirit who could most benefit from what I had to give. Since I didn't get an immediate answer, I put the clothes in a big black garbage bag and placed it in the front seat of my car. In the bag was my Denver Broncos sweatshirt that had some paint on it, but I thought someone would get great joy out of.

Knowing that I would be guided, as I went about my errands I noticed a homeless woman who was devouring a hamburger, licking all of her fingers and even licking the wrapping. She wasn't wearing a coat or a sweater and it was cold outside. So I reached into the bag and pulled out my Denver Broncos sweatshirt along with other clothes I thought would fit her. I went over to her and asked, "Would you like these things to keep you warm?" She looked up at me with a big smile and said "Sure!"

The following Christmas, I was driving down Main Street with a friend to our Church's Christmas Eve rehearsal. I had just told her about giving away my Broncos sweatshirt, when right in front of us was that same woman, wearing my Broncos sweatshirt accompanied by a great big smile. That just made my Christmas! It was loving kindness that boomeranged right back to me. My heart opened with such love. "Maybe Christmas doesn't come from a store. Maybe Christmas means a little bit more."

The gift is in the giving. Our lives are not about taking and hoarding, for those acts are tremendously constricting. Don't you feel a bit contracted when you are trying to get, grab and obtain? Give of yourself, be kind, loving and thoughtful, and you will experience your heart open wide.

Let me share with you a very special Christmas story about an African missionary who worked in what was then known as the Belgium Congo. The missionary told the native people the Christmas story and about the wise men—how the wise men traveled thousands of miles on foot from Babylonia and walked for more than two years in their search for the Christ child. He told them about the gifts of gold, frankincense and myrrh, but he explained that the real gift was the walking so many miles for two years.

Among those who heard the story was a young man by the name of Cungo. One day, Cungo disappeared from his tribe and was gone for more than two weeks. He finally returned with a gift for the missionary, a beautiful necklace. In the middle of the necklace was a gorgeous shell. The missionary asked Cungo where he found that shell and said, "I have never seen such a shell in my whole life." Cungo replied, "I have walked to the Great Sea, and it is only in the Great Sea that this shell is found."

The long walk was the true gift. The long walk is the gift of one's self. The long walk is your gift of loving kindness. Giving of yourself even with small gestures, a smile or a kind word can make all the difference. One act of loving kindness and thoughtfulness is like magic. It opens limitless doors to human connection. Being kind can be very contagious. You give of yourself and are kind to a few people, those people are kind to other people and on and on, in an ever widening kindness circle. That is how it is with kindness.

Remember, all things being connected, every act of kindness no matter how large or small causes a reverberation of positive energy that is felt by the entire world! Martin Luther King didn't just sit back and say, "Somebody ought to do something about the civil rights." Gandhi didn't say, "No way. How could one little Indian transform a nation?" These individuals recognized that each person has the power to make a difference.

Keep loving kindness and thoughtfulness at the forefront of your awareness. More valuable than a shell found in the Great Sea, more valuable than gold, frankincense and myrrh, more valuable than any material thing you could possibly imagine, is the gift of one's self in love and kindness. That is what Christmas is all about.

"Maybe Christmas doesn't come from a store.

Maybe Christmas means a little bit more."

52.

The Prayer of Jabez

When was the last time God worked through you in such a way that you knew without a doubt that it was God? In fact, when was the last time you saw miracles happen on a regular basis in your life? Did you know there is a prayer that has helped many to receive astounding blessings in their lives?

Prayer is where true action is. Prayer is the only action you can take that truly makes things different inside and out. Prayer releases the highest form of energy in the Universe as it links you with God energy, your Source.

As Catherine Ponder puts it so eloquently in *The Dynamic Laws of Prayer*, "When you pray, you stir into action an atomic force. You release a potent spiritual vibration that can be released in no other way. Through prayer you unleash a God energy within and around you that gets busy working for you and through you, producing right attitudes, reactions and results. It is your prayers that recognize and release that God power and God's blessings."

I so agree with her! And the specific prayer is found in 1 Chronicles 4:9-10. Now just to give you a little background, the first nine chapters of 1 Chronicles is taken up with the official family tree of the Hebrew Tribes, a long list of more than 500 unfamiliar names. Not exactly the most exciting part of the Bible, but as you read through the names, you come to a little story after about 44 of those names.

> *"Now Jabez was more honorable than his brothers, and his mother called him Jabez saying, "Because I bore him in pain." And Jabez called on the God of Israel saying, "Oh, that You would bless me indeed, and enlarge my territory, that Your hand would be with me, and that You would keep me from evil, that I may not cause pain!" So God granted him what he requested."*

That's it. That's all there is, the only thing ever said in the Bible about Jabez. Yet there is so much in this simple story that is of value to us!

In this prayer, we see that things started out badly for Jabez, given that his mother named him "Jabez," which means pain. Jabez prayed an unusual, one sentence prayer and things ended extraordinarily well for him. Clearly, something about Jabez's simple yet direct request to God changed his life and left a permanent mark on the history books of Israel as well as in the countless lives of those who have since prayed that prayer.

Can you imagine if your name was "Pain"? My late grandfather, whom we called "Poppy," came from a family of 22 children. He was second to the last, and his mother named him "Hassle." What must have it been like for him to go through life being called "Hassle"! Jabez's beginnings weren't exactly the start of a promising life. But Jabez believed in a God of miracles, so he asked for one. He prayed the biggest, most incredible request imaginable, "Oh, that you would bless me indeed."

The word "indeed" as used in this context means "immensely." Today we would interpret "bless me indeed" as, "Father bless me, and what I really mean is bless me a lot, bless me immensely!" That may sound selfish, but it is not. God really does have unclaimed blessings waiting for you, and it is His loving desire to give them to you. When we seek God's blessing as the ultimate value in life, we are throwing ourselves entirely into His will and His Divine plan for us. When you ask God to bless you and bless you immensely, your life becomes filled with miracles, because you are praying for exactly what God desires for your life. "It is your Father's good pleasure to give you the Kingdom." [Luke 12:32]

The first practical guideline is simply this, pray for God's blessing every day. Which is to say, ask! Ask for God's blessing, directly, explicitly. Sometimes we forget to do this. When we go into a time of prayer, we hold long dissertations with God, and we forget to ask. Even though there is no limit to God's blessings, if you do not ask, you probably won't receive. Don't let a day go by when you might miss out on an incredible blessing just because you didn't ask.

The second part of Jabez's prayer asks that God enlarge his territory. "Enlarge" means to abundantly increase. In Hebrew, the word enlarge actually means "a huge expansion." "Territory" means not only your material territory, but your influence as well. Your territory encompasses your work place, your home environment, your friends, your family and those you only see from time to time. This prayer is not only asking for a gain in material prosperity, but also an expansion in your service, your ministry, as it were, to others. It includes within it a request to sharpen your skills or enable you to do something more effectively.

Your territory is usually not self-initiated, but God-directed. As you let go to God's higher plan, you'll find that God's plan is always greater than what you could imagine.

A couple I counseled used this prayer consistently and with profound faith. They found that their prosperity, in terms of their real estate business and finances, expanded immensely. But along with that, the couple was guided to become mentors for the Big Brothers/Big Sisters organization, an expansion in service, which brought them even greater rewards. God's territory for you is not limited. It is limitless. When you pray this prayer, watch for who and what God will send into your life. It will truly amaze you.

The next sentence in Jabez's prayer is, "That your hand would be with me," meaning that God's power and His grace is with you, that they work on your behalf. There are times when you will just shake your head in amazement and say, "Look what Spirit did!"

My friend Susan and I were driving late at night through the mountain roads of Colorado where I lived at the time. There were no lights anywhere; it was raining hard. We stopped at a stop sign, not sure whether to continue or turn back. Suddenly we got a strong feeling that we should continue and "go and go quickly." As we navigated the winding roads, a rockslide crashed onto the road, right in front of us! We swerved and barely missed being buried. We ran over a boulder, and only just managed to get the car up and over it. We continued to drive home, and when we finally pulled into Susan's garage, the car died and fluid gushed all over the floor. We had made it home just in time.

I realized later that night that the hand of God was with us. Somehow, we were guided to go faster than we would have ordinarily. If we had not, we would have been right in the middle of a rockslide. God's power and Grace was with us.

Jabez's concluding request in his prayer is: "Keep me from evil, that I may not cause pain." What did Jabez mean by this? The word "evil" in Hebrew means pain. What we focus on is what will manifest. If you are focusing on the darkness of the world, the "evil" or "pain," not only do you contribute to it, but such focus will also cause pain or discontent in your life, whether it be emotional discontent, mental discontent, physical discontent or even spiritual discontent.

We are constantly bombarded with negativity—in the news, gossip, even in advertisements that deliberately seek to create discontent, all of which entice us to think negatively about things. What Jabez is saying here is, "Keep me from the world's temptations so that I do not 'cause pain,' as in contribute to the discontent, the darkness, to negativity of any kind.

Jabez was blessed simply because he refused to let any obstacle, person or opinion loom larger than God's ability to bless. Follow Jabez's example. Put God first in all that you do. Put

Him first in your thoughts, words and actions, and you will be protected from the world's temptations.

This prayer has all the components required to bring you fulfillment in every area of your life. Remember, it is God's desire to release His power and Grace in and through you and your life. I suggest you say this prayer for 30 days, and with that, you will be amazed at how God works through you in such a way that you will know without a doubt that it was God.

"Oh, that You would bless me indeed, and enlarge my territory, that Your hand would be with me, and that You would keep me from evil, that I may not cause pain!"

Amen.

My Gift to You

Much as I experience my sermons as gifts from the Universe to me, I hope that you have experienced this book as a gift, one which I delight in sharing with you. It is my fondest desire that the keys you have found within have helped you to to change your course in life where needed, to see Light in the dark places, and to be called into your greatness, for such are truly Spirit's gifts.

May this book hold magic for you, and like a time-release capsule, slowly release its potency, healing and challenging you along your path. May it support and encourage you, so that your life is filled with joy, love and peace!

Rev. Cathy Jean Norman

CATHY JEAN NORMAN graduated from Unity Ministerial school in 1983, and went on to get two Master's degrees—one in Theology from the Peace Theological Seminary & College and the other in Spiritual Psychology from the University of Santa Monica.

After 36 years of Ministry, now retired, Rev. Cathy has served in churches including Christ Church Unity in San Diego, Unity of Delray Beach in Florida, Unity On The Avenue in Denver and Unity of Ventura in Southern California. She also assisted at Unity of The Mountains in Avon, Colorado as well as Unity of Evergreen, Colorado. Currently she is on the speaking circuit at various churches and events.

Rev. Cathy lives in a little Shangri-La-type town called Ojai in California with her husband Steve, and their dogs Pippa and Frankie. Rev. Cathy and Steve love to travel and explore this marvelous planet we call home. You can find out more on her website Sundayfamilydinner.tv.

Dr. Noelle C. Nelson

NOELLE C. NELSON, PhD is a psychologist, trial consultant and author. All of her fourteen books focus on empowering individuals to be happier, healthier and more successful in their personal lives, at work, at home and in relationships. She is a monthly contributor to *Sixty & Me* and regular guest on *HitchedMag* podcasts. She is also a screenwriter: *My Daddy Is In Heaven* was released in 2018.

Dr. Noelle holds advanced degrees in clinical psychology from the United States International University, and sociology degrees from the University of California at Los Angeles and the Sorbonne, Paris. Dr. Noelle's books include *The Power of Appreciation: The Key to a Vibrant Life, Your Man is Wonderful,* and *Happy Healthy...Dead: Why What You Think You Know About Aging Is Wrong and How To Get It Right.* Her interest in happy, healthy longevity led to her popular Facebook page, @ MeetTheAmazings, which celebrates dynamic, thriving, inspiring 60+ers.

Whenever she can, Dr. Noelle indulges her love of reading and travel, but her true passion is dance, from jazz dancing to ice-dancing, to square dancing, and her greatest joys—ballet and ballroom. Find out more at www.NoelleNelson.com, and on Facebook, @MeetTheAmazings, @Dr.NoelleNelson.

Made in the USA
Las Vegas, NV
13 March 2021